Little Foodie

RECIPES *for* BABIES & TODDLERS *with* TASTE

MICHELE OLIVIER

with Sara Peternell, MNT

SONOMA
PRESS

Little Foodie

To Elliette and Parker. Thank you for being my adorable foodies (and critics) from day one. —MO

To Clay and Molly. Thank you for being my patient, sweet, and hungry little guinea pigs. —SP

CONTENTS

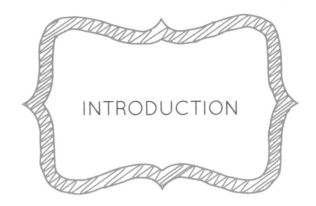

INTRODUCTION

HELLO, MY NAME IS MICHELE, and I am a complete control freak—which I am working on, thank you very much. I am also a lover of food, of course.

I wish I could tell you I always planned to make baby food for my first child, but that would be a lie. I *did* plan to give my little one only the best, which is why I purchased three different brands of organic apple purée to conduct my own quality control.

I tasted each one.

I threw away each one.

Okay, I tossed the jars in the recycling bin. But the point is my love of food made it very clear that what I'd just eaten was not food as I knew it. And I certainly didn't want this to be my daughter's first experience with what the food world had to offer.

I went to the market and grabbed pounds of fresh organic fruits, vegetables, spices, and herbs. Fittingly, my first acts of frenzied baby food making took place at my own mother's house. We started off with simple recipes based on the produce in season. Because my goal was to make purées that tasted better than just "good"—they had to be amazing—I added pinches of spices and herbs to enhance the natural flavors of the produce: apples with cinnamon, sweet potatoes with rosemary, and carrots with nutmeg. The result was more than 800 ounces—yes, you read that correctly—of flavorful, delicious purées. We're talking about half a year's worth of purées. Can anyone say borderline obsessive?

My baby ate them, my husband and I ate them, and I believe (though I cannot say for certain) that Julia Child would have eaten them, too.

Thus began a truly life-changing experience: making baby food for Ellie. More than a hobby, it became my mission, and something I realized I could—and should—share with other parents who hoped to raise children on the full flavors of fresh foods.

Not long after I began creating and testing recipes, I started to blog about them. My "Baby Food for Ellie" concept got shortened to simply "Baby FoodE," and my online recipe home is now fully established at *babyfoode.com*. And sure enough, a little foodie is just what Ellie (now an older sister to baby Parker) has become.

I came to discover it doesn't take that much time or energy to make your baby a foodie—or future foodie, as the case may be. All you really need is a couple of hours each month and a passion to give your baby the best.

This book is the collection of recipes I developed for my babies (and now yours, too). Rest assured, they can be made regardless of how much time you have and how little sleep you're running on. The recipes also deliver big on flavor, and cover everything from memorable first purées to equally memorable (but perhaps less enjoyable) sit-down meals with your feisty toddler. All recipes are both baby- and parent-approved, so you may happily and confidently cook them for many years to come. Enjoy!

PART I

BABIES ARE PEOPLE, TOO

The Food You Eat— Smaller

You have been eating by yourself for as long as you can remember, but the responsibility for feeding another can seem like a lot to take on. If you are a food lover, however, this actually presents an incredible opportunity to acquaint your baby with the wonderful world of food. Passing on your own culinary passion can create a special bond between the two of you, surrounding this activity with great joy and pleasure, as you introduce your child to new and exciting flavors, textures, and aromas from the earliest days.

Think of this chapter as an introduction, or small reassurance, that the food you will feed your baby is (almost) exactly the same food that you eat yourself—just puréed. Healthy fruits, vegetables, proteins, and grains puréed until smooth is all it takes to fill a baby's tummy. Toss in some herbs, spices, healthy fats, and maybe even a pinch of unrefined salt, and your child will not only have a full tummy but a happy one that will (hopefully) lead to a lifetime of healthy eating.

Why We Eat

There's nothing especially interesting about why we, as humans, eat. The most obvious reason is that food sustains our bodies. The nutrition we gain from food keeps us alive, but it also keeps us healthy, active, and alert. The food we eat directly impacts the way we live, and a diet filled with healthy, unprocessed, and colorful food will make us feel better in our day-to-day lives.

But there's a more interesting motivation behind why we eat—and it's not because the sushi told me to. You and I, if I can be so bold, think of food as a force, as something that can transform a meal into a revelation or a bite into the best experience we've ever had. Food is, or can be, truly extraordinary.

Factors ranging from where and how we grow our food, to how, with whom, and for whom we cook it change the simple act of eating from something we need into something we desire. When you lead a lifestyle capturing the true beauty and excitement of food, eating becomes more than just a necessary function—it becomes a true pleasure, one you want to share with others. When guests come to our home, we know which meals will have them talking for weeks. When we decide to eat out, we know which restaurants we want to try, or return to, because the experience promises to be amazingly delicious. There is joy in food.

When my daughter Ellie was born, I started researching and reading both international and American cookbooks on how, why, and what to feed her. When it comes to baby food cookbooks, in particular, the discussion usually focuses on the reasons why babies need to eat fresh fruits, vegetables, and eventually proteins to develop their growing bodies. None of this is frivolous advice or information (and I'll discuss which of this I believe is important a bit later in this chapter). That said, it is rather obvious stuff.

The topic, however, that never came up in any of my readings is how to teach your baby to truly enjoy food: its taste, texture, bright colors, and smells. Attempting to transmit the joy of eating, and sharing the love of food with your baby can be more complex than simply feeding her the same old food every day. It is a passion that takes some planning, patience, and perseverance, but doing so can lead to an incredibly fulfilling adventure.

Thinking about the joy that food can bring fuels me when I'm in the kitchen preparing meals for my family. It encourages me to experiment, take risks, and be flexible, even when something doesn't turn out as I expected. I want my daughters to be healthy, of course. But I also want them to appreciate all that I value about food. If you do, too, let's get going.

Why We Cook

It's easy to buy food for your baby, and many brands now tout that their baby food purées, pouches, and snack bars are organic. Given that you do have a choice, why should you cook at home?

The first reason I began making my own baby food purées was simple (and previously noted)—I am a control freak. But it was only after I had gotten under way producing the purées that I actually began to thoroughly research. The more I read, the more I realized that not only was I making food that tasted far better than store-bought versions, I was also preparing food that was more nutrient dense and less expensive. On top of that, I had complete control over what went into my purées—the ingredients and spices—as well as their texture. But allow me to go into more detail.

TASTE

Nothing tastes better than a healthy, homemade meal, and that goes for baby purée as well. Food always tastes better using fresh ingredients. Yet most commercial baby food purées are heated to extremely high temperatures so they can last upward of three years on the shelf, which means the food you spoon into your little one's mouth is most likely older than your baby. While the convenience of store-bought purées seems ideal for those times you are in pinch, this industrial process kills off most of the flavors, nutrients, and aromas of the produce going into them, leaving purées that taste bland and unnatural.

TEXTURE

The ability to control the thickness of your baby's purée is a tool that will not only help you get though the picky-eating days, but also help transition your baby from purées to solid food. Whenever my daughter would get bored with a smooth purée,

I would simply chunk it up a little. Different textures are as new to your baby as the tastes themselves, so varying a purée's texture will not only give her a new eating experience, it will also tantalize her taste buds.

NUTRITION

There is no debating that homemade baby food is healthier for your baby than any brand of store-bought food, whether jarred or in pouches, but the biggest nutrition win I feel you get for making your own purées is that you can tailor them to your child's needs at any particular moment. Is your baby feeling a little under the

BABY FOOD AROUND THE WORLD

The menu de jour includes fermented soybeans mixed with cabbage; kabocha squash; grilled salmon; green peppers with dried fish; an assortment of sheep, cow, and goat cheeses; and don't forget a big heaping spoonful of fish oil—all served before 8 a.m.! To your toddler! Yup, this is what breakfasts around the world look like. The majority of young children in other countries start their day with a savory breakfast of fish, eggs, fermented vegetables, juice, a porridge of mushy grains, and sometimes even coffee.

Parents who want their kids to grow up and be adventurous eaters, take note: babies whose first bites of food vary in taste and texture will not scoff at eating interesting and varied meals as they grow. Some early meals around the globe include the following:

- In China, babies' first purée is typically a blend of rice, fish, seaweed, and eggs.

- In Jamaica, a custard of apple, mango, banana, papaya, and naseberry is given to babies at four months.

- In Central America, parents spice things up by giving their babies a serving of fruit with a sprinkle of chili powder and lime.

- In India, babies are introduced at six months to a flavorful dish of rice, lentils, and vegetables, spiced up with cumin, coriander, mint, and cinnamon.

Evidently, babies throughout the world are exposed to a wide variety of tastes and textures before they can walk, crawl, or even sit. (And if your mouth isn't watering by now, this is the wrong book for you.) Bland rice cereal be gone!

weather? Make a purée high in vitamin C. Low on iron? Add some beef, spinach, or beans. Maybe your baby is a little constipated. Making a purée with anything that starts with a "P"—pears, prunes, peas, peaches—will soon get your little one back on track. Baby food that is working for your baby's well-being is truly a thing of beauty.

QUALITY CONTROL

Since you're the one who buys the ingredients and handles, preps, and cooks the purées, you can rest assured that you know exactly what's going into all of your baby's food. What you make is what you get! There are no fillers, thickeners, suspicious ingredients with names you can't pronounce, shelf stabilizers, or unnecessary water. By making your own purées, you can also prepare them as you like. Whether you spice it up or chunk it up, you have complete control.

COST SAVINGS

This might come as a surprise to you, but making your own baby food with all organic ingredients is more than 50 percent cheaper than buying the store-bought counterpart. Even though this wasn't my main motivator, it does help the budget if your little one is anything like mine and packing away upward of 25 ounces a day. All of that food gets expensive, and mama can always use a new pair of shoes! Buying produce in bulk from farmers' markets and produce that's in season is a great way to save even more. If it's out of season, frozen produce provides another option for getting the produce you want at a reasonable price.

What We Cook

Your choice to make your own baby food should make you proud. It's a rite of passage for both you and your baby, a milestone to enter in their baby book and post on social media. The ingredients you decide to use in this first purée can vary depending on where you live. In some countries, babies' first food might be a purée of fish and fermented soybeans, while in others it could be a simple leek purée, or in others a purée of robust lentils, cumin, and ginger. I like to find a middle ground in my approach, but my theory is the same: feed babies delicious food and they will continue to eat delicious food as they grow. It's as simple as that. Take encouragement knowing that from a worldwide standpoint, there are actually very few foods completely off limits to infants during their first year (see list on page 21). And whether you decide to start with rice cereal or liver purée, fish or red pepper purée, or even puréed avocado, don't be afraid to add spices and herbs—this not only improves the flavor of your baby's food but adds beneficial medicinal properties.

ALL OF THE INGREDIENTS

Traditional wisdom regarding nutrition has changed over the years. According to the American Academy of Pediatrics, your little foodie can eat almost everything right from the beginning. Keeping this in mind, you don't have to bother following a rigid schedule of food introductions as long as your basic list of ingredients contains fresh, whole foods. Better yet, you don't have to hold off on using certain items just because they might seem too advanced, too exotic, or too sophisticated.

THE PAST In the not-too-distant past, pediatricians recommended what could be considered a cautious and bland approach to food introductions. Parents were largely advised to offer rice cereal as a first food and to delay the introduction of herbs and spices, citrus fruit, eggs, peanuts, fish, and so on for fear of babies having allergic reactions. But a lot has changed in the last seven years. The American Academy of Pediatrics now notes on its healthychildren.org website that there is no medical evidence showing that the introduction of nutrient-dense foods (such as fish and well-cooked eggs) after four to six months of age has any effect on whether your baby will be allergic to them. The same website also points out that "For most babies it does not matter what the first solid foods are." As a result, holistic nutritionists and savvy pediatricians now recommend a combination of real, whole food ingredients as the most nutritious choice for your baby's first foods.

For those families where there is a history of allergy or food sensitivity, some caution should be taken. In Chapter 2, there is a section (see page 33) dedicated to explaining more about allergies, intolerances, and digestive troubles when introducing food.

THE PRESENT Unless there is a family history of allergies, a baby can eat almost anything right from the start. Feel free to begin with fruits and vegetables, which are perfect for your baby's first taste. Ripe and ready banana or avocado offer the total package: convenient, a good source of vitamins and minerals, high-fiber content, and delicious flavor!

Protein and fat play a critical role in development as well, so take note of the following facts on foods offering a healthy dose of each.

Protein is found in a number of foods, not just from animal sources. Of course, tuna, shrimp, turkey, cod, snapper, venison, halibut, salmon, scallops, chicken, lamb, beef, liver, and eggs are animal-based foods. However, plant-based foods like

spinach, mustard greens, crimini mushrooms, lentils, split peas, kidney beans, black beans, pinto beans, and garbanzo beans are all great sources of protein as well.

Fat should not be feared. Children need high levels of fat throughout their early growth and development. Fats provide energy and also help children build muscle and bone. In addition, fats help assimilate the fat-soluble vitamins A, D, E, and K, necessary for protein and mineral absorption as well as hormone production. Choose a variety of healthy fats such as butter, coconut oil, avocados, and olive oil, and of course, the healthful fats that naturally accompany quality animal sources, once your baby is ready.

SEASONAL, ORGANIC, AND LOCAL

Whenever possible, I prefer to use seasonal, local, and organic ingredients, as produce in season is filled to the brim with the most intense, juicy flavors. No surprise, these ingredients yield purées with the most rounded and bold flavors, too. But in many parts of the country, this isn't feasible year-round. So then the debates start: organic over local or seasonal over organic. This can go on and on. Rule of thumb, use the best that's out there. Start with organic whenever possible or affordable (sorry $9 organic strawberries—not going to happen), and if possible, go local and seasonal. Usually local and seasonal go hand in hand. Farmers' markets, Community Supported Agriculture (CSA), and boxed food services offer great affordable produce options and are popping up in every city around the country. Get to know the ones in your neighborhood and ask if they spray (that is, spray pesticides on) their produce. You'll find that many local farms that aren't "certified organic" do in fact have organic practices in place. It's simply that the process of certification is too costly for many producers.

SEASONAL Nothing is better than biting into a sun-ripened, juicy-to-perfection piece of fruit. A summer peach or winter orange has a taste that simply cannot be replicated. Since seasonal produce is picked at the peak of ripeness, it will be packed with both nutrients and flavor. In effect, seasonal produce is like a bomb of flavor, so by making purées with fruits and vegetables in season, you are giving your baby a culinary experience that will be forever engraved in her sensory memory. But while we tend to think of the summer months as the ones with the best seasonal produce, don't discard the off-seasons for interesting varieties of produce. Winter brings squash, pears, and turnips; fall produces pumpkin, Brussels sprouts, and mushrooms; while with spring we get fennel, mangos, and green beans.

JUST SAY NO: FOODS TO AVOID

The world of foods open to babies is more expansive than ever before, but it's still advisable to hold off on a number of items—some for 12 months, others indefinitely. More information on allergies is explained in Chapter 2 (see page 33).

BEFORE 12 MONTHS:

- **Honey** Honey can contain botulism spores, which an infant's digestive system is not equipped to handle. After 12 months, babies' bodies are developed enough so that they're not compromised by such a threat.

- **Choking hazards** Foods that present a choking hazard, such as hard or raw vegetables, popcorn, grapes, and nuts.

- **Refined grains** The refining process eliminates the nutrients in grains, leaving only the white, starchy carbohydrate behind.

- **Foods that a family member is allergic to** Avoid introducing foods to which an immediate relative (parent, brother, sister) has a known anaphylactic food allergy—that is, an allergy that causes a severe reaction upon exposure, such as itching, hives, or trouble breathing. A few foods commonly triggering such reactions include peanuts; tree nuts like almonds, walnuts, and cashews; or finned fish like salmon or tuna. Seek guidance from your pediatrician on the best time to introduce such foods.

INDEFINITELY (AS BEST YOU CAN)

- **Processed dairy** Processed dairy products are filled with artificial flavors and colors, and high quantities of sugar. Yoplait's popular Go-Gurt contains a whopping ⅔ of the daily recommended amount of sugar for children. Meanwhile, processed cheeses like Kraft Singles and Velveeta are similarly produced with food coloring and sugar, plus saturated vegetable oils.

- **Commercially prepared fruit drinks** Only buy juice labeled 100 percent juice, and avoid so-called "blends" containing small amounts of a variety of fruits like apple, grape, and pear. Most juice blends are actually full of water, sugar, and other additives, with very little nutrients. In fact, most contain less than 10 percent real juice.

- **Commercially packaged foods with hard-to-pronounce ingredients on the label** Processed meats like hot dogs, salami, and other lunch meats include nitrites, food coloring, high levels of sodium, and dubious flavor enhancers. Popular packaged products like Pepperidge Farm Goldfish and Nestlé Nesquik Chocolate Milk contain refined ingredients that are best to avoid from infancy through adulthood!

ORGANIC Given the rise of public concern over health issues involving pesticides, added hormones, and genetically modified foods, the organic food industry's popularity has soared over the last couple of years. You can now find a section dedicated to organic food at almost any supermarket across the country.

Organic foods are simply defined as foods grown in their natural state without the use of synthetic chemicals—pesticides, fertilizers, herbicides, and fungicides—and without the addition of antibiotics or growth hormones. They also cannot be genetically modified organisms (GMO). In order to receive the USDA label for "organic," the food must be grown according to a set of strict rules.

Since a baby eats more produce per pound of food than adults, starting your baby on a diet of organic produce is best. If this is too cost prohibitive, then it's important to get to know the Dirty Dozen and the Clean Fifteen (see page 217 for lists of each). The Dirty Dozen includes the fruits and vegetables that have the highest levels of pesticides when grown conventionally. I always pass on buying fresh produce that's on the Dirty Dozen if I can't find or afford it organic. The Clean Fifteen includes the fifteen fruits and vegetables that are grown with very little pesticide, so they're considered "clean" and okay to buy if you can't find or afford organic. These lists are here to help us make good and healthy decisions for our children, taking into account that it's not easy to buy organic every time.

But wait—there is one more great option: the frozen foods section at the supermarket or even big box stores like Costco. Frozen organic foods have been a game changer for me. Not only are they reasonably priced, they are flash-frozen at the height of freshness, providing top-quality organic produce all year-round.

LOCAL As the local farming scene continues to explode in most areas, getting local produce is becoming a feasible—and even convenient—option for many families. By visiting your local farmers' markets, or joining a CSA or community farm, you are not only reducing your carbon footprint but supporting local businesses. (It's a bonus that most farmers' markets provide coffee trucks for those of us parents surviving with very little sleep!) Another option for getting local produce is to grow it yourself—nothing will help build a healthy relationship between your child and their food like getting those chubby little hands dirty growing their own fruit, vegetables, and herbs. Some of my favorite childhood memories come from eating strawberries, carrots, and raspberries straight from the vine, dirt included. Don't have the space in your backyard for a garden? Check if you have a community garden nearby.

Innovative websites, such as www.fallingfruit.org and www.pickyourown.org, are popping up in cities that offer opportunities for crop sharing and pick-it-yourself locations. Crop sharing is for people who grow their own produce but end up with more of a particular item than they can use; local websites help them get in touch with others who've grown too much of different items, and they share. We participated in this system last year with our peaches. We have a glorious peach tree that produces hundreds of peaches a year, and even after the neighborhood moms and I hosted a toddler picking party, I still had enough peaches to trade for a bunch of organic, local apples. A real win-win for both parties.

Then there are pick-it-yourself websites. These help you locate local trees in public places or people who grow produce (mostly fruit) on their properties—as long as you pick it yourself, the produce is free to take.

What *We* Eat

Growing in popularity is a school of thought that babies should begin their culinary adventure by eating, well, exactly what we eat—and skipping the purée stage altogether. According to this belief, babies' first foods should not be cut into small bites—which indeed could be choking hazards—but large pieces they can hold onto, lick, mash into their faces, and, before long, bite and swallow. This is commonly referred to as baby-led weaning (BLW), but a clearer way to describe the approach is baby *self-feeding*.

I have included a very long chapter of purée recipes in this book that I think are just fantastic, so it's pretty obvious I haven't personally practiced BLW with my own little ones. But if it piques your interest, here's some basic information worth considering.

PROS

The pros, I admit, are pretty compelling.

- The baby eats what the family eats.

- You don't need extra time to make food just for your baby.

- You can eat your own meal while it's still hot, because you're not spending that time feeding your little one.

If you're preparing a roast with a side of broccoli for your family, steam the broccoli for your baby, and lay it on the highchair tray. Large pieces of banana, cucumber (peeled), ripe mango, and toast fingers all make for worthy early food introductions. But there's no rule against starting with what's on your own plate, too. Scoop some mashed potatoes onto your child's highchair tray, or a two-to-three-inch slice of grilled steak.

Letting babies learn to self-feed is said to give them the freedom to explore new tastes and textures without the pressure of having to eat a set amount of food. At the same time, this process allows babies to choose what, how much, and how quickly they want to eat, promoting a healthier bond to food and a willingness down the road to eat everything and anything.

CONS

There is much debate within the BLW community about the cons I note below. The good news is that you can find a lot of information online, including videos on YouTube, to guide you in deciding whether or not BLW is something you'd like to try.

CHOKING For many parents, the biggest concern with BLW (actually, the same worry whenever you decide it's time to introduce chunky finger foods) is that the baby may choke on pieces of food. While babies might gag or cough a bit when learning how to self-feed, the fact is they have a very strong anti-choking reflex. In most gagging cases, babies will be able to correct it on their own before help is needed, but it is always a good idea to have an infant-child CPR class in your back pocket for worst-case scenarios (and your own peace of mind).

MESSES Yes, since your baby will have complete control over her food, this method is going to be messier than the spoon-fed approach. But this has an easy enough fix: buy a plastic mat for under the high chair, a good bib with a catch-all attached, and paper towels—lots and lots of paper towels.

ALLERGIES While allergies and intolerances are a concern for every parent, with BLW, the baby is able to eat multiple foods at once without the common four-day wait period between foods. While this may be liberating for many people (myself included), take caution if you have any major food allergies in your family.

As I've explained, exposure to flavors at this young age is more important than consumption, and BLW is very much in line with this thinking. I also strongly believe that, from a very young age, babies and adults are capable of enjoying the same foods, and that adults should be able to enjoy "baby food" as well! For those who want to skip right over purées, this book provides plenty of finger and snack food recipes to start with right away if you'd like to try the BLW approach. I find a great way to incorporate this method with purée feeding is to offer a baby a solid food to pick up and explore by herself, while simultaneously spoon-feeding her a serving of purée. When she gets the hang of feeding herself, you can also use purées as a fun dip. Think of this as the best of both worlds.

If BLW sounds like a good fit for you and your family, I encourage you to look into it further and read Gill Rapley's book *Baby-Led Weaning* for more information.

Raising a Food Taster

Let's get real. Your baby, toddler, and kid aren't going to eat every delicious dish you put in front of them. They are going to toss aside some of the dishes you make especially with them in mind and devour the meals you thought they would never touch. They are going to keep you on your toes, that is for sure. However they react to your prepared meals, don't let this derail you from your goal of raising a Food Lover. It takes time. It takes patience. It takes a repeated and often painful persistence. The thing to keep in mind is that you are not going to have a Food Lover at the beginning.

FOOD TASTER → FOOD EATER → FOOD LOVER. GOT IT?

From the first bite and first meals you are simply attempting to raise a Food Taster, a little foodie superhero who isn't afraid of anything—green, sour, lumpy, or cold, she will try it all. This Food Taster will evolve into a Food Eater, a toddler who you'll pray will go against the norm (on most occasions) and eat whatever you put in front of her. Realistically, this stage of the game is going to be the toughest: toddlers will push food away, demand something else, and sometimes be downright mean about it. There will be ups and downs (and what will sometimes feel like complete circles), but don't give up; your goal is almost in sight—the final outcome of raising a Food Lover, a child who will happily eat, and even prefer, healthy and flavorful meals made with varied spices, unique textures, and exotic flavors from different cultures . . . most of the time.

The "How-To" Chapter

I have no doubt that this chapter will be similar to those stroller directions you tossed aside until you couldn't for the life of you figure out where that extra bolt goes. This "How-To" chapter is just that: a chapter you will skip until one day you are in the kitchen blissfully making three different purées and suddenly realize you have no idea how to go about storing them, or—more importantly—how to actually feed them to your baby.

How to Know When Your Baby Is Ready for Purées

There is no particular age when your baby will be ready to start eating purées. It just doesn't happen like that. Age takes a backseat to the signs your baby gives you herself as to her developmental readiness. While pediatricians generally recommend introducing solid food around six months of age, it's more important that before starting your child on solids you can answer "yes" to most of the following questions:

- Can your baby sit up on her own?
- Is your baby able to hold her head and neck in an upright position?
- Does your baby reach for, or eye, your food while you are eating?
- Is she hungry more often and not satisfied after finishing her usual amount of breast milk or formula?
- Has her weight doubled since birth?

If those questions generate a mix of yes and no answers, it's no big deal. Just wait a bit. Babies live the lives we adults often wish we could—they do what they want, when they want, no matter what anyone else wants or expects. Your baby might not be ready, even if all of her baby buddies have been eating for months. Your baby might give you all the right indications, but she could absolutely reject her first purée (without a care for all of the love and excitement you put into it, I might add). And you can be sure she won't be ready when your mother-in-law visits and wants nothing more than to feed her grandchild herself.

Start when the signs are there, and continue to keep trying. At some point, your little one will be ready, and she will open her mouth to her very first bite of food.

How to Introduce Purées

High chair? Check. Bib? Check. Fully charged cell phone? Check.

With this holy trinity of baby-feeding accoutrement, you're ready for that first feed.

The faces, oh, the faces your baby is about to make. Out of all the firsts, feeding was the most fun—and the messiest. So grab a few wipes, double-check that your phone has enough storage for dozens of photos and videos, and let's get started.

Before you begin, make sure your baby has a little bit of breast milk or formula in her belly: about half of what you'd normally give in a regular feeding. Not too full. Not too hungry. Just right. It's also good for you to have a little food in your own belly. Being "hangry" (the very serious condition in which the state of hunger is so severe that one is driven to anger) isn't good for anyone.

THE PRINCIPLES

This is not going to be a clean and simple process. Your baby may eat food one day, refuse it the next, and paint her face with it the next. It's all okay. Playing with her food is a good thing; it is simply a way for her to explore, learn, smell, and taste the world around her. So have those wipes close by, and remember:

- Start slowly. Two teaspoons, once a day, is enough food for babies the first couple of meals. Their bodies need time to adjust and digest this new food. If they are still acting hungry, give them some more breast milk or formula.

- Let the baby decide. Your little one should determine the pace of how fast or slow she wants to eat.

- All spoons on deck. Have more than one spoon ready. Your baby will surely snatch one out of your hands to play with, which is a-okay.

- Have fun. Smile at your baby throughout the experience, and try to relax. The more fun you have, the greater the likelihood your baby will enjoy it too (even if she barely eats or doesn't eat at all).

After a couple of days, you can build up the quantity of food you offer one table-spoon at a time.

THE IDEAL

When you're ready to start the feeding, select a purée you've already made, place just one or two teaspoons of it into its own bowl, and slightly warm this small amount. You can choose whether to gently spoon it into your baby's mouth or hand the spoon over to her to attempt self-feeding. If your baby tries to grab the spoon from you and get it into her mouth by herself, whoa—you've got a success on your hands. If the experience is a bit milder, and she lets you spoon some purée into her mouth, enjoy it. This is a winning experience, too.

HOW TO FREEZE, STORE, AND THAW PURÉES

Your freezer is about to become your new best friend, allowing you to keep several weeks' worth of baby purées at the ready.

FREEZE

Whenever you make a purée, put several ounces in the fridge for your little one to enjoy that week, then freeze the rest of the batch for her to finish up at a later date.

After making your purée, let it cool slightly and then transfer to ice cube trays, glass canning jars, or BPA-free containers made for storing baby food. I prefer using ice cube trays so you can serve small portions of purée in the beginning, or have the freedom to mix and match different cubes to create new and interesting combinations.

Cover the ice cube trays with the provided lid or plastic wrap, and place in the freezer. Let them freeze completely before you crack the purées out of the trays and place them in plastic freezer bags. Label and date each bag.

STORE

All purées in this book can be stored for three to four days in an airtight container in the fridge. If freezing them, my rule of thumb is that most produce-based purées can last up to three months in the freezer (avocados and bananas are an exception), while all purées containing meat, beans, or grains will last two months in the freezer.

THAW

Thawing may seem like a no-brainer, but it never hurts to know your options. There are three different ways to thaw purées:

Microwave Take the purée cubes that you want to serve out of your freezer, place them in a glass container, and microwave in 20-second increments, stirring every time. The purée is ready when it is just warm to your touch.

Grab two clean spoons, one for you and one for your baby, and test your purée before serving.

Some infants like their purée cold, warm, or really warm, and some will devour it no matter the temperature. You will get to know your baby's personal preferences as the two of you bond over food.

Fridge This one takes the longest time, but it is a great alternative to using a microwave.

Take the purée cubes you want to serve out of your freezer, and place them in glass containers with airtight lids.

Leave in the fridge for 12 to 16 hours. Do not leave the purée in the container to thaw on the counter or anywhere out of the fridge, as bacteria will start to grow at a rapid rate—definitely not good.

The purée will be cold but thawed, so if your baby likes her purée warmed, you'll have to finish the job using the microwave or stovetop method.

Stovetop In the smallest saucepan you can find, place the purée cubes you want to serve, and gently thaw them on medium-low heat until warm, stirring occasionally.

THE LIKELY

Some babies will simply not open their mouths. Some babies will take one bite, clamp their mouths, and turn away. If (and when) any of this happens, don't force the spoon into their mouth, and don't stress out. Here are a couple of things to try:

- Put a bit of the purée on the end of your finger and see if your baby will suck it off. This is an unintimidating way to begin, especially as spoons can be scary for little ones.

- Pour a tablespoon onto the high chair tray, and allow your baby to play with it, if she wants. This is a less managed approach to letting the baby explore new food. As babies love to put everything in their mouths, odds are at least some will get in (or near) it.

If your baby has no interest in these options, end the feeding. Dispose of the one or two teaspoons you warmed, and put the remaining, unheated purée in the refrigerator to try again tomorrow.

Remember that before their first birthday, babies receive their main source of calories, vitamins, fat, and protein from your breast milk or formula. At this point, any purées you give them are just for fun, mainly to get them used to eating and exploring real food.

How to Introduce New Foods

Your baby has tried her first purée and is loving it—or at least she's letting you spoon it into her mouth and giving you a perplexed look. Either way, this is a great start. After three or four days of feeding her the first purée, it is time to work in some new ones.

While there are several different methods regarding which foods to introduce first, my approach is as follows:

- Start your baby on a purée made with lots of fruits and vegetables. Color, color, color!

- Slowly mix those purées with fat and protein from naturally raised, hormone- and antibiotic-free animals or fish.

- Sprinkle in some ancient grains (quinoa, millet, or barley) straight from the source, not processed from a box.

ALLERGIES, INTOLERANCES, AND DIGESTIVE TROUBLES, OH MY

The beauty of the reigning nutritional wisdom is that it expands the field of foods we can offer our little ones. At the same time we need to pay attention to how our children react to these foods and proceed or pivot based on what happens. Your own intuition and wisdom should guide you when it comes to what your baby needs to grow, thrive, and stay healthy in the first year of life. Still, there are a few things to consider on this topic.

ALLERGIES

A person with an anaphylactic food allergy has a severe, potentially life-threatening reaction that can occur within minutes or even seconds of exposure to the allergen and requires an injection of epinephrine and sometimes even a trip to the emergency room. According to the Mayo Clinic, these "true" food allergies are actually found in only 5 percent of the population. Among this small percentage of people, the foods they most commonly react to include:

- peanuts
- nuts
- fish
- wheat
- dairy
- citrus
- tomato
- egg whites

If you are aware of a close relative (mom, dad, sibling) with a true food allergy, consult your doctor, and make a plan for introducing these foods around 12 months, not earlier.

INTOLERANCES

While food intolerances and sensitivities do not cause an anaphylactic food reaction, they are still quite troublesome when it comes to symptoms. Intolerances to wheat, gluten, dairy, soy, corn, and other foods often result when the body is unable to break down or digest a particular food.

Can we prevent these intolerances? During pregnancy, you can take probiotics and digestive enzymes as supplements to improve the digestive health of both you and your baby. Later, if you notice your child is experiencing digestive problems, you can give her infant-specific strains of probiotics.

If you're already aware of your own sensitivity to grains such as rice or wheat, you may want to hold off introducing them to your child until after the 12-month mark. Sally Fallon, in her heralded whole-foods cookbook *Nourishing Traditions*, noted that waiting to introduce grains can help reduce the likelihood of developing food intolerances and belly complaints in general. In this book, only a handful of the recipes for 12 months or younger include grains.

DIGESTIVE TROUBLES

An infant's digestive tract is, understandably, immature for a good part of the first year of life. This is why so many babies suffer from gastrointestinal discomforts such as gas, spitting up, constipation, and loose stools, especially when introducing foods. Just remember, babies can have slight reactions to foods while trying new ones, but this doesn't mean they are allergic to those particular foods or that we should stop feeding them solid food altogether. Just give it some time.

ONE PURÉE AT A TIME

While you will probably want to jump-start your baby's culinary adventure with the fun combination recipes in this book, it's a good idea to start with single ingredient purées. Allowing your baby four days between introducing new foods will give you time to spot any allergies or reactions your little one may have (read more about allergies on page 33). I find it best to switch back and forth between fruits and vegetables for babies' first foods. After you have confirmed she is not allergic to any of the foods you have given her, you can start to mix and match single purées into different and exciting combinations.

If baby doesn't seem to care for a certain purée, don't let this discourage you. Simply, put that one away for a couple days and try again later. It can take a baby up to 15 different tries before she decides whether she likes a certain fruit or vegetable.

The most important thing to remember is that for the first months of feeding, all you are providing is an atmosphere of learning and fun—you are helping your baby learn to eat, chew, and swallow new foods while developing and tempting her palate with texture and taste, using different produce, spices, and herbs.

How to Transition from Purées to Solids

Your baby is a rock star. She is eating all (or at least most) of your delicious combinations with vigor and can't seem to get enough. This makes you a rock star as well. After you have patted yourself on the back for a job well done, it's time to move on and help baby transition from purées to solids. You got it right—your work as a parent is never done.

IS YOUR BABY READY FOR SOLID FOOD?

Again, there is no magic age when your baby will be ready to begin eating solid foods. This transition generally takes place around nine months of age, but you'll know, simply by watching and listening to her subtle clues:

- She refuses to eat off a spoon unless she has complete control over it.
- Her pincer grip has developed, and she can get most foods to her mouth by herself.
- She can eat thicker, chunkier purées without a problem.
- She can easily mush food around in her mouth with her gums.

Now that your baby is ready for solid foods, there are a couple of ways to ease her transition.

CHUNK IT UP The first method is to continue with the same purées you are already making, just in a chunkier consistency. Start slowly by adding a small amount of chunk in an otherwise smooth purée. As your baby adjusts to thicker purées, you can make them chunkier.

- **Pulsing:** Instead of blending your purées into a smooth consistency, two to three quick pulses in the blender or food processor will allow you to adjust the thickness to your baby's taste.

- **Smashing:** Take your freshly cooked recipe and smash it down with a fork or potato masher until you reach your desired consistency.

- **Increase in Size:** Increase the size and quantity of grains, meat, and beans you include in your purées until you finally have incorporated the full item.

Once your little one has mastered eating these chunkier purées, you can simply offer chunks of small and mushy food alongside the chunky purée, always giving them the option of what type of food they prefer.

GOOD STARTER SOLID FOODS

The key here is to offer your baby small pieces of mushy, steamed, soft, or cooked foods to prevent any choking hazards. Start with small pea-size pieces of solid food, and work your way up in size.

- Pieces of hard-boiled egg yolks
- Pieces of ripe banana, avocado, mango, peaches, or blueberries
- Cooked apples or pear chunks
- Steamed carrots, peas, corn, beets, sweet potato, or yellow squash
- Cooked pasta: ziti, bowtie, or orzo work best
- Cooked cubes or ground pieces of chicken, fish, or tofu
- Soft cheese: mozzarella, goat, or cream cheese
- Cooked beans that are soft and cut in half: black, cannoli, or garbanzo

STRAIGHT TO SOLID FOODS The second approach is to just go straight from purées to solid food, skipping the chunky purées altogether—some babies want to use their fingers to eat and be done with purées completely. However, I would recommend offering a purée alongside solid foods to make sure your baby always has a food option she likes.

SOLID FOODS AT SNACK TIME Another great way to introduce solid foods to your baby is to offer them at snack time. Purées at meals, solids as snacks. This gives a baby the opportunity to eat with her hands without all the pressure of making it happen at mealtime.

Some babies will be more interested in playing with their finger food than eating it. Expect a mess: it will get all over her, your new carpet, and most definitely your new shirt. It's all okay. After some time and practice, your little one will get better at getting it into her mouth and less interested in tossing it at you. Remember: Keep it fun. Keep it social. Keep it interesting.

How to Use This Book

Okay, it's true, you don't really need me to tell you how to use this book. It is—and should be—pretty obvious. But a few features, I think, are important to call out, to help you get the most value out of this book.

The recipes on the following pages will have age flags, but they're not age ranges, per se. You'll see 4+ months, 6+ months, 9+ months, and so on. The idea is that you should know when you can start to feed your baby certain recipes, but there really is no top end to the range. Your baby's purées aren't for her alone—they can be dips, or sauces, or even soups for you. Many recipes include tips to help you make the most out of them or adapt them further. There are even a handful of tips for cocktail, wine, and beer pairings with family meals to help you, well, not mind so much when your baby simply sniffs at your food, and no more. Yes, there's something for everyone in here.

Beyond those specifics, there are a few things I'd like to share with you—on a more personal level, kind of like a *Little Foodie* handshake.

- **Growing:** The recipes in this book are broken down into four different chapters, beginning with purées and ending with family meals. It's a book that grows just as your little one does—from a baby, to a toddler, and into a big kid.

- **Forgiving:** If you don't like an ingredient in a recipe, just change it. These recipes are forgiving in that way. Your family doesn't like chicken? Switch it with beef or fish. Your toddler despises everything green? Add some red bell peppers instead. Even though these are my tried-and-true recipes, they are never set in stone. Each time I make them I often change something myself depending on what is in season, what I have on hand, or (usually) what I forgot to pick up at the store.

- **Approved:** Every recipe in this book has been enjoyed by me and my family from the minute my little one was able to eat. They have all been approved by my own little taste tester, who, despite my best efforts, still has her super picky toddler days (or weeks).

- **Loved:** This book is meant to be lovingly used, filled with notes, dog-eared, colored in, splashed with wine, dropped, and otherwise abused until the spine is ripped off and found in a basket of spit-on toys.

- **Fun:** The recipes in this book are here to motivate and inspire you. You are in charge of how your baby learns to eat, which can seem overwhelming, but can also create a wonderful way for your family to spend memorable, quality time together in the kitchen. Food (and life) is supposed to be fun, messy, and chaotic. So let's roll up our sleeves and get cooking.

TOP 5 HERBS + SPICES

These are my go-to favorites, and I always keep them well stocked. While each one has a distinct taste, they are all well-rounded enough to enjoy in almost any purée.

Remember that dried spices and herbs can go bad with age and exposure to direct sunlight, so try to buy (or grow!) and use fresh as much as possible. While I do recommend using fresh herbs whenever possible, dried herbs can be a great substitute.

SPICES

- Cinnamon
- Cloves
- Nutmeg
- Curry
- Cumin

HERBS

- Basil
- Cilantro
- Thyme
- Mint
- Rosemary

A general rule of thumb: 1 teaspoon of dried herbs = 1 tablespoon of fresh herbs

PART II

RECIPES FOR ONE & ALL

Purées

(4+ MONTHS)

Frequently Asked Questions

Is it okay to add spices to my baby's first purées?

There's no nutrition-based rationale for your baby to endure plain, tasteless mush. Breastfed babies have already had a taste of their mother's diet, as breast milk takes on the flavors of food eaten by the mother. Although formula-fed babies haven't had the same exposure to flavors, first foods with spices and herbs make for wonderful introductions. Even mildly spicy food doesn't have to be off limits. Babies in other parts of the world have thrived on flavorful, spicy food for generations. But hold the jalapeños, of course.

Will my baby get enough iron if I don't use iron-fortified rice cereal?

Yes. *The Journal of Nutrition* reports that iron-rich foods that supported the mother during pregnancy also pass to the baby through breastfeeding. Research suggests that a breastfeeding mother with optimal iron status provides sufficient iron stores to her baby for at least six months, so additional supplements shouldn't be needed, unless a blood test indicates otherwise. Formula tends to come iron-fortified, which gives your child a good base as you supplement formula with solid food.

Instead of feeding your child iron-fortified cereals (which are heavily refined and lack other nutrients found in whole foods) or iron supplements (which many pediatricians still recommend), you can easily boost your baby's iron by making your own baby food from iron-rich foods. "Heme" iron (the most absorbable form) is found in animal foods, so a diet rich in pasture-raised eggs, poultry, and grass-fed beef and dairy will help maintain your baby's iron stores.

Are there certain foods that will make my baby gassy?

A little bit of gas is no big deal and quite common when introducing solid foods, because your baby's digestive system is working harder to break down new and more complex foods. Your baby's system matures quickly in her first year, and you will witness fewer tummy troubles as you continue to introduce additional foods. A number of other factors may be causing gas as well. Consider the following: How quickly is she eating? Is she gulping air with every bite of food? How much is she eating? Does she have an intolerance to this particular food?

My baby keeps eating and eating her purées—can a baby eat too much?

Your baby's tummy is the size of her fist, so technically, that is all she can hold! Babies come with a sophisticated self-regulation system: When she's hungry, she will eat. When she's full, she'll stop. However, many of the first foods you give her (like puréed fruits and vegetables) digest rapidly, so she may continue eating past fullness, as the contents of her stomach empty before the meal is even complete. Trust your baby's instincts for feelings of hunger and fullness. Letting her decide how much to eat is setting the stage for a lifelong healthy relationship with food and her body.

Here's a purée with zing right from the start. Apples are a common first food, and with good reason—babies love their mildly sweet taste, and the high fiber content is easy on a young digestive system that's adjusting to new foods. Meanwhile, cinnamon adds a kick irresistible to both babies and adults. This recipe will grow with your little one: try a smooth purée for baby's first food, a smashed one for a toddler meal, and a go-to chunky applesauce for your big kid.

Apples + Cinnamon

4+ MONTHS

MAKES 20 ounces
PREP TIME: 10 minutes
COOK TIME: 15 minutes

STORAGE
Refrigerator: 3 days
Freezer: 3 months

6 apples, such as Fuji, Gala, or Pink Lady, peeled (optional), cored, and chopped into quarters

½ cup water

¼ teaspoon ground cinnamon

In a medium saucepan, add the apples, water, and cinnamon. Cover and heat on medium for 10 to 15 minutes, until the apples are tender. They will be done when you can cut the quarters in half with a wooden spoon. Let them cool slightly.

Place all the ingredients into a blender or food processor, and purée until you reach your desired consistency.

TIP Make your baby a smarty-pants by adding cinnamon here, there, and everywhere. Just breathing in the smell of this wonderfully sweet spice boosts brain activity!

Bugs Bunny got it right about this magical root vegetable: carrots *are* divine, making a bright, nutrient-loaded purée. With a heaping dose of beta-carotene, iron, and vitamin A, this smooth and tasty purée helps develop skin, bones, teeth, and vision. Adding nutmeg brings out carrots' earthy and robust flavors and downplays any potentially acidic undertone.

Carrots + Nutmeg

4+ MONTHS

MAKES 25 ounces
PREP TIME: 10 minutes
COOK TIME: 15 minutes

STORAGE
Refrigerator: 3 days
Freezer: 3 months

2 pounds carrots, peeled and chopped into small pieces

¼ teaspoon ground nutmeg

1 cup water (reserved from steaming), breast milk, or formula, divided

Fill a medium saucepan with about 2 inches of water. Heat on medium until the water begins to boil.

Place the carrots in a steamer basket over the boiling water, and cover for 7 to 10 minutes, or until the carrots are tender. Let them cool slightly.

Place the carrots and nutmeg into a blender or food processor, adding liquid in ¼ cup increments, until you reach your desired consistency.

TIP This mild purée mixes well with a variety of other purées, such as pear, apple, beet, cauliflower, sweet potato, butternut squash, and even banana. Have some fun and mix it up.

Smooth, delicate, and not overwhelmingly sweet, pears are a gold ribbon winner in my book. When slightly heated, pears can be whipped up into a fluff-like purée for your baby. While my favorite simple purée matches mild pears with bold cloves (and is spooned over Greek yogurt), pears can also be paired with carrots, chicken, spinach, white fish, or oats.

Pear + Cloves

4+ MONTHS

MAKES 20 ounces
PREP TIME: 5 minutes
COOK TIME: 10 minutes

STORAGE
Refrigerator: 3 days
Freezer: 3 months

6 pears, peeled, cored, and chopped
    into quarters

½ cup water (reserved from
    steaming), divided

¼ teaspoon ground cloves

In a medium saucepan, add the pears, water, and cloves. Cover and heat on medium for 10 minutes, stirring occasionally, until the pears are tender. They will be done when you can cut the quarters in half with a wooden spoon. Let them cool slightly.

Using a slotted spoon, scoop the pears out of the saucepan, leaving any extra water behind. Place the pears into a blender or food processor. Reserve ½ cup of water.

Purée the pears until you have reached your desired consistency, adding reserved cooking water in ¼ cup increments if needed.

TIP Ripe pears are a great first finger food for baby. Simply peel and cut into 2-inch-long pieces so your baby can grab and chew (or mush) these soft pear sticks with her gums.

The three musketeers of purées: peas, zucchini, and mint! Alone, each of these is just not right—peas a little overwhelming to a baby's sensitive taste buds and belly, zucchini a little bland, and mint too strong. But when they come together, this trio is smooth, creamy, and impossible to resist. All for one, and one for all!

Peas + Zucchini + Mint

4+ MONTHS

MAKES 15 ounces
PREP TIME: 5 minutes
COOK TIME: 10 minutes

STORAGE
Refrigerator: 3 days
Freezer: 3 months

2 medium zucchini, trimmed, and
    roughly chopped

2 cups peas, fresh or frozen

8 mint leaves

Fill a medium saucepan with about 2 inches of water. Heat on medium until the water begins to boil.

Place the zucchini in a steamer basket over the boiling water, and cover for 5 minutes. Take the steamer basket of zucchini out of the medium saucepan, and set aside. Let them cool slightly.

Add the peas to the leftover hot water in the medium saucepan for 3 to 5 minutes.

Place the zucchini, peas, and mint leaves in a blender or food processor, and purée until you reach your desired consistency.

TIP Minty, cooling, fresh! An essential culinary herb for maintaining a healthy digestive tract, mint assists digestion and helps your baby absorb nutrients. Gas, nausea, and tummy pain can all be relieved by a pinch of mint.

Dense with nutrition and sweet in flavor, sweet potatoes are a perfect food for your baby. Versatile to no end, they're perfect for Mom, too. You can steam them, roast them with some olive oil, chop and bake them for an easy finger food, not to mention pair them with a plethora of spices: nutmeg, cinnamon, curry, cloves, cumin, cilantro, rosemary, or thyme, just to name a few. This recipe creates a tasty combination of creamy and sweet with just a touch of spice that will leave your baby's taste buds clamoring for more.

Sweet Potato + Coconut Milk + Coriander

4+ MONTHS

MAKES 20 ounces
PREP TIME: 5 minutes
COOK TIME: 50 minutes

STORAGE
Refrigerator: 3 days
Freezer: 3 months

3 medium sweet potatoes or yams

½ cup canned coconut milk, full fat

½ teaspoon ground coriander

Preheat the oven to 400°F.

Prick the sweet potatoes several times with a fork and place on a baking sheet. Roast in the oven for 45 to 50 minutes or until tender. Let them cool slightly.

Peel away the skin, and place the sweet potato flesh in a blender or food processor.

Add the coconut milk and coriander, and purée on high for 1 minute or until smooth, adding additional coconut milk if needed.

TIP Besides being delicious, coconut milk contains a significant amount of healthy, plant-based, saturated fat. One component of this fat is lauric acid (a compound also found in mother's milk), which has been shown to promote brain development and bone health.

The first time Ellie tasted guacamole, it wasn't this baby-style version; it was the standard adult kind she snatched from right under our noses—jalapeños and all. The look after her first spicy bite was priceless! While I have no problem introducing a baby to slightly spicy foods, full-on spicy guacamole may not be the best idea for a first purée. Filled with healthy fats, a smooth, irresistible texture, and a zesty taste, this baby "guac" is milder than the restaurant variety and a perfect starter purée for your baby.

Avocado + Cilantro

4+ MONTHS

MAKES 4 ounces
PREP TIME: 2 minutes

STORAGE
Refrigerator: 2 days

½ avocado

3 cilantro leaves, finely chopped

¼ lime, juiced

Cut the avocado in half, remove the pit, and scoop out the flesh.

Mash the avocado, cilantro, and lime juice together with a fork, or place all ingredients into a food processor or blender, and purée until smooth. Serve immediately.

TIP As your baby grows, so can this purée. Feel free to mix in cumin, tomato chunks, garlic, pineapple, corn, black beans, and even a dash of hot sauce for a more true-to-form guacamole. Serve to your baby with a spoon, and enjoy yourself with chips.

While cauliflower can be bland by itself—I call it the tofu of vegetables—roasting it with flavor-bursting tandoori, a seasoning mix featuring coriander and cumin, creates an ethnic purée worthy of your taste-craving baby. Though this recipe is ultimately for a purée, the preblended roasted cauliflower florets here are perfect for your baby when she starts eating finger foods.

Cauliflower + Tandoori

6+ MONTHS

MAKES 25 ounces
PREP TIME: 5 minutes
COOK TIME: 30 minutes

STORAGE
Refrigerator: 3 days
Freezer: 3 months

½ head of cauliflower, chopped into florets

2 apples, cored and roughly chopped

½ teaspoon tandoori seasoning

Preheat the oven to 400°F. Line a baking sheet with parchment paper or a silicon mat.

Place the cauliflower and the apple pieces on the baking sheet, and lightly sprinkle with the tandoori seasoning.

Bake for 20 to 25 minutes or until the cauliflower is tender and can be pricked with a fork.

Let cool slightly.

Transfer the cauliflower and apple into a blender or food processor. Purée until smooth.

TIP Tandoori is a spice blend from eastern India typically used on roasted chicken. Cumin and coriander are the main spices, but the blend can include smoked sweet paprika, turmeric, garlic, and ginger. Most grocery stores will stock it in the spice or ethnic food section.

The first time I made this recipe was actually for myself. After all, moms need special treats, too! Thick, rich, and dangerously easy to eat, this purée is roasted to the point of no return and sprinkled with cinnamon and a pinch of Himalayan salt. It will haunt your sleep-deprived dreams until you make another batch . . . for your baby, of course.

Roasted Blueberry + Himalayan Salt

6+ MONTHS

MAKES 10 ounces
PREP TIME: 5 minutes
COOK TIME: 10 minutes

STORAGE
Refrigerator: 3 days
Freezer: 3 months

1 cup blueberries

½ teaspoon ground cinnamon

Pinch Himalayan salt

Preheat the oven to 400°F. Line a baking sheet with parchment paper.

Place the blueberries on the baking sheet, and sprinkle with cinnamon. Bake for 10 minutes, and stir halfway through cooking time. Let cool slightly.

Place the blueberries and Himalayan salt in a blender or food processor, and purée until smooth.

. . . .

TIP For my favorite mama treat, spoon a giant serving of the purée over vanilla bean ice cream, find a quiet spot, sit back, and enjoy. You deserve it!

. . . .

Red bell peppers might seem like an unusual first purée, but when gently steamed, this bright and colorful vegetable turns mildly smooth with just a little tang. When paired with a drizzle of olive oil, this purée promotes your baby's bone growth, prevents tummy troubles, and is easy on the taste buds. Healthy fats not only provide nutrients but also boost flavor.

Red Pepper + Olive Oil

6+ MONTHS

MAKES 15 ounces
PREP TIME: 5 minutes
COOK TIME: 15 minutes

STORAGE
Refrigerator: 3 days
Freezer: 3 months

1 small white potato, peeled and roughly chopped

2 red bell peppers, cored, seeded, and roughly chopped

1 teaspoon extra-virgin olive oil

1 cup water (reserved from steaming), breast milk, or formula, divided

Fill a medium saucepan with about 2 inches of water. Heat on medium until the water begins to boil.

Place the potatoes in a steamer basket over the boiling water, and cover for 10 minutes. Add the red peppers to the steamer basket, and cook for an additional 5 minutes. Let them cool slightly.

Place the potato, red peppers, and olive oil in a blender or food processor; reserve steamed water, if using; and purée, adding liquid in ¼ cup increments if needed, until you reach your desired consistency.

TIP This purée can serve as a great simple soup for the rest of the family as well. With a dollop of crème fraîche, a drizzle of olive oil, and a sprinkle of thyme, this "soup" can became part of a family dinner, pleasing everyone around the table.

Tough on the outside, tasty on the inside, pumpkins make a perfect first food. This pumpkin purée is slightly sweet, somewhat savory, and majorly addictive and will become your little one's new go-to meal for fall.

Pumpkin + Thyme

6+ MONTHS

MAKES 30 ounces
PREP TIME: 5 minutes
COOK TIME: 60 minutes

STORAGE
Refrigerator: 3 days
Freezer: 3 months

1 small pumpkin, such as pumpkin pie variety, seeded, guts removed, and chopped into quarters

½ teaspoon dried thyme

1 cup water, breast milk, or formula, divided

Preheat the oven to 350°F. Line a baking sheet with parchment paper or a silicon mat.

Place the pumpkin pieces on a baking sheet, skin-side down.

Roast for 45 to 60 minutes or until tender, and the pumpkin pieces can be pricked with a fork. Let cool slightly.

Peel away the skin from the flesh, and place the pumpkin in a blender or food processor. Add the thyme and purée, adding liquid in ¼ cup increments until you have reached your desired consistency.

TIP Fresh thyme contains one of the highest antioxidant levels among herbs, making it a powerful agent in preventing disease and promoting health. In a world bombarded by environmental and food pollutants, it's reassuring to know you can add thyme to your baby's meals for an extra dose of wellness.

For an unexpected twist on apple purée, add some mint! This purée combines sweet and smooth with fresh and cool—a perfect pairing. While you can stop with just apples and mint, by mixing these ingredients with rich and creamy ricotta cheese, you add yet another surprise to tantalize your baby's taste buds. Ricotta is an ideal cheese for a baby: full of calcium and protein, yet low in salt.

Apples + Mint + Ricotta

6+ MONTHS

MAKES 15 ounces
PREP TIME: 5 minutes
COOK TIME: 15 minutes

STORAGE
Refrigerator: 3 days
Freezer: 3 months (add the ricotta after thawing)

4 apples, Fuji or Pink Lady, peeled (optional), cored, and chopped into quarters

½ cup water

6 mint leaves

2 tablespoons whole-milk ricotta cheese, divided

In a medium saucepan, add the apples and water. Cover and heat on medium for 10 to 15 minutes, stirring occasionally, until the apples are tender. They will be done when you can cut the quarters in half with a wooden spoon. Let them cool slightly.

Place the cooked apples and mint leaves in a blender or food processor. Purée, adding water until you reach your desired consistency.

Add the ricotta cheese to just the amount of purée you are planning to serve or refrigerate, and pulse until all ingredients are incorporated.

TIP Other great protein-rich dairy mix-ins for this purée include cottage cheese, Greek yogurt, goat milk yogurt, or kefir.

Bursting with flavor, this purée is a perfect sweet treat for any time of day. Serve for breakfast with a spoonful of yogurt, pair with a butternut squash purée for a sweet and savory combo, or finish the day with this purée after a hearty green meal.

Peach + Strawberry + Vanilla Bean

6+ MONTHS

MAKES 20 ounces
PREP TIME: 5 minutes
COOK TIME: 15 minutes

STORAGE
Refrigerator: 3 days
Freezer: 3 months

2 cups peaches, fresh or frozen

2 cups strawberries, fresh or frozen

¼ cup water

½ vanilla bean pod, cut lengthwise, seeds scraped out and reserved

In a medium saucepan, add the peaches, strawberries, and water. Cover and heat on medium for 10 to 15 minutes, stirring occasionally, until the peaches are tender. They will be done when you can cut the quarters in half with a wooden spoon.

Add vanilla bean seeds, and cook for 1 to 2 more minutes. Let them cool slightly.

Using a slotted spoon, scoop out the peaches, strawberries, and whatever vanilla bean seeds adhere to them, leaving excess water in the saucepan. Place in a blender or food processor, and purée until you reach your desired consistency.

TIP Because both peaches and strawberries are on the Dirty Dozen list, I would recommend using fresh or frozen organic peaches and organic strawberries here.

This purée was actually inspired by a peach and fennel salsa I tasted when visiting a restaurant in Nashville. It sounded so crazy I just had to try it—it turns out, pairing fennel and peach creates magic in the mouth! The sweetness of the peach calms down the spice of the fennel, and their combination produces an unforgettable taste experience I just had to re-create for my baby.

Fennel + Pea + Peach

6+ MONTHS

MAKES 15 ounces
PREP TIME: 5 minutes
COOK TIME: 10 minutes

STORAGE
Refrigerator: 3 days
Freezer: 3 months

1 fennel bulb, white part only,
    roughly chopped

2 cups peaches, fresh or frozen

1 cup peas, fresh or frozen

Fill a medium saucepan with about 2 inches of water. Heat on medium until the water begins to boil.

Place the fennel in a steamer basket over the boiling water, and cover for 5 minutes. If using frozen peaches or peas, add to the steamer basket with the fennel, and steam for an additional 5 minutes. Let them cool slightly. If using fresh peaches or peas, place directly in a blender or food processor.

Place the fennel, peaches, and peas in a blender or food processor, and purée until you reach your desired consistency.

TIP For a grown-up peach and fennel salsa, combine ½ cup diced fennel; 2 cups peeled and diced peaches; 1 cup diced, roasted red bell peppers; ½ cup diced red onion; 1 minced garlic clove; and a pinch of salt and pepper in a medium bowl. Place in the fridge, and let chill for 30 minutes before serving with your favorite chips.

Cherries and apricots really shouldn't be friends: cherries hog attention while apricots prefer to play it cool, flying somewhat under the radar in the stone fruit world. But when these two are thrown together in the oven, they mingle in a refreshingly complementary way. The addition of freshly grated ginger also helps soothe digestive troubles while adding a pinch of spice and gusto to an otherwise calm purée.

Apricot + Cherry + Ginger
WITH GREEK YOGURT

6+ MONTHS

MAKES 20 ounces
PREP TIME: 10 minutes
COOK TIME: 25 minutes

STORAGE
Refrigerator: 3 days
Freezer: 3 months (add the yogurt after thawing)

12 apricots (or 2½ cups), fresh or frozen, cut in half and pitted

1 cup pitted red cherries, fresh or frozen

1 teaspoon grated fresh ginger

½ cup Greek yogurt, full fat, divided

Preheat the oven to 450°F. Line a baking sheet with parchment paper.

Place the apricots and the cherries on the baking sheet, and bake in the oven for 20 to 25 minutes, or until bubbly and slightly browned.

Scrape all of the fruit and the extra juices into a food processor or blender. Add grated ginger, and purée for 30 seconds or until smooth.

Add 1 to 2 teaspoons of Greek yogurt for every 2 ounces of purée you are planning to serve or refrigerate, and pulse until all ingredients are incorporated.

TIP Apricots are an excellent source of fiber. If your little one ever suffers from a bout of constipation, an occasional occurrence when starting new solid foods, you'll find this a useful recipe for your cabinet of foods-as-medicine.

While we all have our likes and dislikes regarding food, these personal tastes should never influence your baby's eating habits. Broccoli just isn't my thing, but not for a minute did I let that stop me from offering it to my baby girl. To this day, I have to hide my surprise when she reaches into the fridge, takes out a hunk of broccoli, and nibbles on it raw. This purée will help turn any broccoli skeptic into a potential fan: a perfect balance of heavy-duty, nutrient-dense broccoli; creamy, smooth leeks; and spicy chives, this purée is a winner—even to me!

Broccoli + Leek + Chives

6+ MONTHS

MAKES 15 ounces
PREP TIME: 5 minutes
COOK TIME: 10 minutes

STORAGE
Refrigerator: 3 days
Freezer: 3 months

2 cups broccoli florets

1 leek, white and light green parts, roughly chopped

1 teaspoon finely chopped chives

1 cup water (reserved from steaming), breast milk, or formula, divided

Fill a medium saucepan with about 2 inches of water. Heat on medium until the water begins to boil.

Place the broccoli and leek in a steamer basket over the boiling water, and cover for 10 minutes or until the broccoli and leek are tender. Let them cool slightly.

Place the broccoli, leek, and chives into a blender or food processor, reserve steamed water, if using, and purée, adding liquid in ¼ cup increments, until you reach your desired consistency.

TIP Broccoli is a wonderful vegetable enhancing both digestive and immune system health. It contains significant amounts of fiber that assist with digestion, as well as phyto-nutrients that support the body in eliminating toxins. Rich in vitamins and minerals, broccoli may even help reduce allergies and asthma.

Short on time? Try this perfect no-cook purée filled with potassium-rich banana and iron-heavy dried apricots, with just a hint of sassy coriander. While I prefer this as a chunky compote-style purée, you can blend longer for a smoother consistency if your baby isn't yet accustomed to chunkier textures. Using rehydrated dried fruit is a great way to feed babies fruit that's out of season, as well as different textures and tastes to which they haven't yet been introduced.

Chunky Apricot + Coriander

6+ MONTHS

MAKES 5 ounces
PREP TIME: 10 minutes

STORAGE
Refrigerator: 2 days
Freezer: 1 month

5 dried apricots

1 cup boiling water

1 ripe banana, peeled and cut into pieces

Pinch ground coriander

Place the dried apricots into a small bowl. Pour in the water and let them soak for 10 minutes.

Place the banana, apricots, and coriander in a blender or food processor, and pulse until all ingredients are incorporated, and the purée is still chunky.

TIP Coriander wasn't an everyday spice in my pantry before my baby-food-making days, but it has since become a staple for me. With its sweet robust taste, coriander also contains a hint of cloves and citrus that pairs well with almost any mild fruit or sweet vegetable—apricots, bananas, sweet potatoes, carrots, and pears.

Chia seeds are the superfood of the moment, and rightly so—packed with fiber, protein, omega-3 fatty acids, calcium, magnesium, and phosphorus, these little seeds deserve this coveted title. Combining mangos, packed with vitamin A, and creamy coconut milk, this super purée tastes rich enough for dessert but is healthy enough for any meal.

Mango + Chia Seeds + Coconut Milk Pudding

6+ MONTHS

MAKES 10 ounces
PREP TIME: 5 minutes

STORAGE
Refrigerator: 3 days
Freezer: 2 months

1 ripe mango, peeled, pitted, and
    roughly chopped

1 teaspoon chia seeds

½ cup coconut milk

¼ teaspoon vanilla bean extract

Place the mango, chia seeds, coconut milk, and vanilla bean extract into a blender or food processor, and purée until you reach your desired consistency.

Once refrigerated or frozen, this purée might become a little thick, so add additional coconut milk or water if needed.

TIP This pudding is also perfect for a toddler—and for you! Add a drizzle of honey or maple syrup for a touch of sweetness and a couple chunks of fresh mango on top for an extra special snack or dessert.

As vegetables go, green beans are not particularly flashy. They don't have fan clubs or diets centered on them. They don't demand attention, but maybe they should: they are loaded with calcium, manganese, and vitamins K and C, and help prevent a large number of illnesses. That earns green beans rock star status in my book.

Green Beans + Parsley

6+ MONTHS

MAKES 10 ounces
PREP TIME: 2 minutes
COOK TIME: 10 minutes

STORAGE
Refrigerator: 3 days
Freezer: 3 months

2 cups green beans, roughly chopped, fresh or frozen

1 teaspoon dried parsley

1 cup water (reserved from steaming), breast milk, or formula, divided

Fill a medium saucepan with about 2 inches of water. Heat on medium until the water begins to boil.

Place the green beans in a steamer basket over the boiling water, sprinkle with parsley, and cover for 7 to 10 minutes or until the green beans are tender. Let them cool slightly.

Place the green beans and parsley in a blender or food processor, reserve steamed water, if using, and purée, adding liquid in ¼ cup increments, until you reach your desired consistency.

TIP Don't have dried parsley on hand? Fresh parsley will also work. Remember that 1 tablespoon of fresh herbs can be substituted for 1 teaspoon of dried.

This recipe is bliss, pure apple bliss! A simple but decadent purée that tastes like dessert—for mother and baby both! Roasted apples and bananas are caramelized into a rich, thick, and creamy combination reminiscent of warm apple pie. Perfect for when you need a sweet little pick-me-up, this purée is best served warm with your baby close at your side.

Roasted Apple Bliss

6+ MONTHS

MAKES 20 ounces
PREP TIME: 5 minutes
COOK TIME: 30 minutes

STORAGE
Refrigerator: 3 days
Freezer: 3 months

3 apples, peeled (optional), cored, and sliced in quarters

2 bananas, peeled and chopped to same size as apples

1 teaspoon ground cinnamon

1 cup water, breast milk, or formula, divided

Preheat the oven to 350°F. Line a baking sheet with parchment paper.

Place apples and bananas on the baking sheet, and sprinkle with cinnamon.

Bake for 25 to 30 minutes, or until bubbly and browned. Let cool slightly.

Place apples and bananas in a blender or food processor, and purée, adding liquid in ¼ cup increments, until you reach your desired consistency.

TIP For an extra special treat, add blueberries, cherries, or peaches to the baking sheet along with the apples and bananas. Better yet, make a batch of each. Your tummy will thank you.

This purée is like a warm, thick, comforting blanket for those times your baby needs an extra bit of love. Chicken and carrots baked with a little butter and a sprinkle of rosemary produce a smooth caramel-hued purée that will not only warm your baby's belly, but ease his or her pain. While you can pair this purée with a small serving of pasta, I prefer to serve it with a spoonful of barley for extra nutrients.

Comforting Chicken +
Carrot Purée + Rosemary

6+ MONTHS

MAKES 10 ounces
PREP TIME: 5 minutes
COOK TIME: 30 minutes

STORAGE
Refrigerator: 3 days
Freezer: 2 months

1 chicken thigh, trimmed of fat, cubed

4 carrots, peeled and roughly chopped

1 teaspoon butter

¼ teaspoon roughly chopped
   fresh rosemary

Preheat the oven to 400°F.

On a large sheet of aluminum foil, place the chicken, carrots, butter, and rosemary. Wrap them like a package, with the seams facing upward.

Bake for 30 minutes, then let cool slightly.

Transfer all the ingredients from the foil packet to a blender or food processor, and purée until you reach your desired consistency.

TIP To prepare a barley accompaniment, simply bring ½ cup barley and 1¼ cup water or stock to a boil. Reduce heat to medium-low, and simmer, covered, for 40 to 50 minutes, or until most of the liquid has been absorbed. Let stand for 5 minutes, and fluff with a fork.

Pears and oats cook slowly together in this recipe until the oats plump and the pears get soft and supple. With some dates for sweetness (and fiber) and a hint of cloves, this rustic porridge could become your family's favorite for years to come. I started making this porridge for Ellie when she was 7 months old, and even though she's almost 3 years old now, she still insists I make it for her to this day, though not puréed, of course. As she likes to remind me, she's a big girl now.

Rustic Pear + Oat Porridge + Cloves

6+ MONTHS

MAKES 15 ounces
PREP TIME: 5 minutes
COOK TIME: 15 minutes

STORAGE
Refrigerator: 3 days
Freezer: 2 months

2 pears, cored and chopped

¼ cup dry old-fashioned oats

3 dates, pitted and chopped

¼ teaspoon ground cloves

1 cup water

In a medium saucepan, add the pears, oats, dates, cloves, and water. Cover and heat on medium for 10 to 15 minutes, stirring occasionally, until the pears are tender. Let cool slightly.

Place all of the ingredients in a blender or food processor, and purée until you reach your desired consistency.

TIP If your little one has a gluten sensitivity, make sure to use a brand of oats that states they are gluten-free. While oats are naturally gluten-free, they can get contaminated in a processing faculty that also processes wheat, barley, and rye.

As much as I love beets for a baby purée, they can be a "bloody" mess to make, eat, and clean up. This purée uses golden beets as well as mild acorn squash to combat this problem. Still a beautiful sunshine color, this purée contains all the calcium and vitamin A of traditional beets—plus the folate and potassium of squash—without all those nasty red stains. Basil leaf has a very calming effect on the stomach, and when added to your baby's food, it actually helps her digestive system properly absorb nutrients from the meal.

Golden Beets + Squash + Basil

6+ MONTHS

MAKES 25 ounces
PREP TIME: 10 minutes
COOK TIME: 70 minutes

STORAGE
Refrigerator: 3 days
Freezer: 3 months

½ acorn squash, seeded

1 sweet potato

2 golden beets

10 basil leaves, roughly chopped

1 cup water, breast milk, or formula, divided

Preheat the oven to 400°F. Line a baking sheet with foil.

Place the squash, skin-side down, on the baking sheet. Prick the sweet potato several times, and place on the baking sheet. Individually wrap the beets in foil, and place on the baking sheet.

Bake all the vegetables for 45 minutes. Remove the squash and set aside.

Bake the sweet potato and beets for another 20 to 25 minutes or until tender and can be pricked with a fork. Let cool slightly.

Scrape the squash and sweet potato from their skin. Trim and peel the beets.

Place all the vegetables and the basil in a blender or food processor, and purée, adding liquid in ¼ cup increments, until you reach your desired consistency.

When life gives you pit fruit, make pit-perfect purée. Summer is the ideal season to make and freeze as many purées as possible. Each fruit is amazing on its own, but combined, they're a summer taste sensation! Add thyme, which has high antioxidant levels, to your baby's meals for an extra dose of wellness. Warm, juicy, and sweet, with just the right amount of tart, this purée is like eating summer, one bite at a time.

Pit Perfect Purée with Thyme

6+ MONTHS

MAKES 20 ounces
PREP TIME: 5 minutes
COOK TIME: 40 minutes

STORAGE
Refrigerator: 3 days
Freezer: 3 months

2 peaches, cut in half and pitted

2 nectarines, cut in half and pitted

3 plums, cut in half and pitted

3 apricots, cut in half and pitted

¼ teaspoon roughly chopped fresh thyme

Preheat the oven to 350°F.

In a baking dish, place the peaches, nectarines, plums, and apricots, skin-side up.

Fill the baking dish with ½-inch water, and bake for 30 to 40 minutes or until a fork can easily be inserted into all of the fruit. Let cool slightly.

Peel the skin off of all the fruit, and place in a blender or food processor. Add the thyme, and purée until you reach your desired consistency.

TIP Pit produce not in season? Not a problem. Use frozen produce in place of fresh, and you'll get the same delicious results. Place frozen fruit on a baking sheet, and cook for an additional 10 to 15 minutes over the recommended baking time.

This "hummus" was originally intended as a thick, spoon-fed purée for baby. But it was only when I took a taste on a carrot stick (dipped into my baby's bowl) that I realized how versatile it could be: a baby's purée, a toddler's finger food dip, or a yummy afternoon snack for me. Anyway you eat it, this "hummus" is filled with healthy green peas, fiber-filled chickpeas, a zesty splash of lemon, and turmeric—a spice with major proven benefits for your body and brain.

Green Pea "Hummus"

9+ MONTHS

MAKES 2 cups
PREP TIME: 5 minutes

STORAGE
Refrigerator: 5 days
Freezer: Not recommended

1 cup peas, fresh or frozen, thawed

1 cup chickpeas, drained and rinsed

½ teaspoon ground turmeric

2 tablespoons lemon juice

2 tablespoons olive oil

Place the peas, chickpeas, and turmeric in a food processor or blender, and begin to purée.

Slowly add the lemon juice and the olive oil through the top spout, and continue to purée, scraping down sides every so often, until you have reached a smooth consistency.

COCKTAIL PAIRING TIP For the grownups, pair hummus and veggies or crackers with a Lemon Gin Fizz. In a cocktail shaker filled with ice, add 4 tablespoons gin, 1 tablespoon lemon juice, and 1 teaspoon powdered sugar: shake and then strain into a glass filled with ice. Top with club soda, and garnish with a lemon slice.

No little foodie's global purée repertoire would be complete without this Thai beef and broccoli recipe. Filled with a delicious light curry and citrus flavor, while packed with iron and protein, this purée will awaken your baby's taste buds to an array of new spices and textures—not to mention prepare her for all those late-night takeout meals she'll consume in college.

Baby's First Thai Beef + Broccoli

9+ MONTHS

MAKES 25 ounces
PREP TIME: 10 minutes
COOK TIME: 20 minutes

STORAGE
Refrigerator: 3 days
Freezer: 2 months

1 teaspoon olive oil

½ pound beef, cubed

1 cup unsalted beef broth or water

1 orange, juiced

¼ teaspoon red curry paste

2 cups broccoli florets

½ russet potato, peeled and finely chopped

In large skillet, heat the olive oil over medium heat.

Place the beef into the skillet, and brown on all sides for 5 to 8 minutes.

Add the stock, juice, and curry paste to the beef, and deglaze the pan with a wooden spoon. Bring liquids to a slight boil.

Add the broccoli and potato, cover, and let cook for 10 minutes, or until potatoes are tender. Let cool slightly.

Transfer all ingredients to a blender or food processor, and purée until you reach your desired consistency.

TIP This recipe is also great for toddlers: leave whole and serve over steamed brown rice. For a well-rounded meal, serve with a cucumber salad.

Every time I make this recipe, I flash to my high-school days and sing a Rusted Root song, way too loud, completely off key, and making up words as I go along. If for a second you thought I was cool, let's just be clear: I am not. But how can you *not* sing when making this healthy and colorful meal for your little bundle of joy? Sweet potato, parsnip, and carrots are sprinkled with cumin and roasted until just caramelized with goodness, then added to protein-filled quinoa for a chunky purée that will have your baby "cooing" along.

Roasted Root Veggie Purée + Quinoa

9+ MONTHS

MAKES 25 ounces
PREP TIME: 10 minutes
COOK TIME: 45 minutes

STORAGE
Refrigerator: 3 days
Freezer: 2 months

FOR THE PURÉE

1 sweet potato, peeled and
    roughly chopped

1 parsnip, peeled and roughly chopped

2 large carrots, peeled and
    roughly chopped

2 teaspoons olive oil

½ teaspoon ground cumin

1 cup unsalted stock or water

FOR THE QUINOA

½ cup uncooked quinoa, rinsed

1 cup water

Preheat the oven to 350°F. Line a baking sheet with foil.

Place the sweet potato, parsnip, and carrots onto the baking sheet.

Drizzle the vegetables with the olive oil, and toss until everything is well coated. Sprinkle with cumin.

Bake for 30 to 45 minutes, stirring halfway through, or until all vegetables are tender and can be pricked with a fork.

Meanwhile, in a small saucepan, bring the quinoa and water to a boil. Reduce heat to medium low, cover, and let simmer for 15 minutes or until all of the water has absorbed. Set aside, covered, for 5 minutes.

Transfer the baked, cooled vegetables and liquid to a blender or food processor, and purée until you reach your desired consistency.

In a medium bowl, combine the quinoa and the roasted vegetable purée.

TIP Olive oil is one of the best fats for boosting both flavor and nutrition. The mono-unsaturated fat content of olive oil is what makes it a heart-healthy choice for all ages. To retain its healing properties and delicious flavor, it's best not to heat olive oil above 350°F, so be sure to roast those veggies low and slow.

WHAM! POW! BANG! This purée is a superhero, and it will save your day! Loaded with healthy green vegetables, lean protein, and just the right amount of sweetness, this purée is packed with calcium, protein, fiber, vitamin A, and iron—all essential nutrients for the healthy growth and development of your baby. Best of all, it takes less than 30 (mostly hands-free) minutes to prepare, leaving you plenty of time for your other super-parent duties.

Superhero Green Purée + Chicken

9+ MONTHS

MAKES 20 ounces
PREP TIME: 5 minutes
COOK TIME: 20 minutes

STORAGE
Refrigerator: 3 days
Freezer: 2 months

½ chicken breast, uncooked

2 small zucchini, roughly chopped

2 apples, cored and chopped into quarters

2 cups trimmed, packed baby spinach

Fill a medium saucepan with about 2 inches of water. Heat on medium until the water begins to boil.

Place the chicken breast in a steamer basket over the boiling water, and cover for 10 minutes. Flip the chicken, and add the zucchini, apples, and spinach on top of the chicken. Cook for an additional 10 minutes, then let cool slightly.

Remove the chicken to check for doneness, and then roughly chop.

Place all ingredients into a blender or food processor, and purée until you reach your desired consistency.

TIP Buying prewashed, organic packaged baby spinach is a great way to save time in the kitchen while adding some greens to your baby's diet. You can add baby spinach to almost any purée, smoothie, pasta sauce, or pizza.

One of my all-time favorite dishes is homemade risotto filled with a bounty of seasonal vegetables, And while cooking it can be a great excuse to stand still and sip a glass of wine, this technique can be impossible to pull off with two kids demanding attention. In this baby-friendly method, I pulse together precooked brown rice, steamed veggies, a bit of vegetable stock, butter, and lemon for a creamy, tangy risotto that leaves me with free time to play with the kids—with or without a glass of vino in hand.

Spring Green Risotto
WITH LEMON + CHIVES

9+ MONTHS

MAKES 30 ounces
PREP TIME: 10 minutes
COOK TIME: 15 minutes

STORAGE
Refrigerator: 3 days
Freezer: 2 months

3 medium zucchini, roughly chopped

1 apple, cored and quartered

1 leek, white and green parts
    only, chopped

1 cup asparagus, trimmed and chopped

2 cups trimmed spinach

½ garlic clove, minced

2 teaspoons chopped chives

2 cups cooked brown rice

1½ cups unsalted vegetable broth, divided

1 lemon, juiced

1 tablespoon butter

Fill a medium saucepan with about 2 inches of water. Heat on medium until the water begins to boil.

Place the zucchini, apple, leek, asparagus, and spinach in a steamer basket over the boiling water, cover for 10 to 15 minutes or until all of the vegetables are tender. Let them cool slightly.

Transfer the zucchini, apple, leek, asparagus, and spinach to a food processor. Add garlic and chives, and pulse for 2 seconds at a time until all the ingredients are just about smooth.

Add the rice and pulse again for 2 seconds at a time, adding broth in ¼ cup increments, until all the ingredients are incorporated yet still chunky.

Add lemon juice and butter, and gently stir until all the ingredients are incorporated and the butter is melted.

TIP Butter is actually very nutritious, providing your baby with necessary cholesterol, vitamin A, and essential fatty acids. Butter from grass-fed cows is best because it doesn't contain added hormones commonly given to conventionally-raised cattle. More good news: since butter doesn't contain large amounts of milk proteins, it's minimally allergenic.

Ever since I lived in Italy for my junior year abroad, I have held a special place in my heart—and stomach—for authentic Italian food. I made this purée for my daughter in an effort to replicate a bowl of soup I ate in a tiny cafe on a hillside in Tuscany after my first wine-tasting festival: a simple soup of puréed butternut squash and roasted red bell peppers with small white beans, topped with a dollop of fresh cream. While the soup did nothing for my hangover the following day, it created a lasting impression on my taste buds and has since haunted my culinary dreams.

Mumbo Italiano

9+ MONTHS

MAKES 30 ounces
PREP TIME: 5 minutes
COOK TIME: 60 minutes

STORAGE
Refrigerator: 3 days
Freezer: 2 months

1 small butternut squash, cut in half and seeded

1 red bell pepper, seeded and roughly chopped

1 can northern white beans, drained and rinsed

4 sage leaves, roughly chopped

¼ teaspoon ground allspice

1 cup water, breast milk, or unsalted stock, divided

TIP For a chunkier consistency, purée half the beans with the butternut squash and the red pepper, then purée the remaining beans after.

Preheat the oven to 400°F. Line a baking sheet with foil.

Place the butternut squash on the baking sheet, skin-side down, and roast for 45 to 60 minutes, or until tender and the skin can be pricked with a fork. Let cool slightly.

Meanwhile, fill a medium saucepan with about 2 inches of water. Heat on medium until the water begins to boil.

Place the red pepper in a steamer basket over the boiling water, and cover for 10 minutes. Let cool slightly.

Scrape the butternut squash from the skin, and place in a blender or food processor. Add red pepper, beans, sage, and allspice, and purée, adding liquid in ¼ cup increments, until you reach your desired consistency.

Wowzers! This coconut curried lentil purée is good! I made it for my baby, but ate it for my own lunch instead—right out of the blender. I'm talking seriously yummy here. This earthy vegetarian purée is loaded with fiber, iron, and protein, and can be served smooth or chunky. I like to introduce it as a smooth purée, then reserve some of the lentils from the pot, adding them back in after I blend the rest of the ingredients for some additional thickness. Serve with toasted pita and a sprinkle of cilantro for a more grown-up meal.

Put the Lentil in the Coconut

9+ MONTHS

MAKES 20 ounces
PREP TIME: 5 minutes
COOK TIME: 20 minutes

STORAGE
Refrigerator: 3 days
Freezer: 2 months

1 teaspoon olive oil

¼ yellow onion, finely chopped

1 teaspoon grated fresh ginger

2 carrots, peeled and chopped

1 sweet potato, peeled and chopped

½ cup dry red lentils, washed and picked over

1 teaspoon mild yellow curry powder

1½ cups unsalted vegetable stock or water

½ cup coconut milk

In a medium saucepan, heat the olive oil over medium heat.

Cook the onion for 5 minutes or until translucent. Add the ginger and stir for 1 minute.

Add the carrots, sweet potato, lentils, curry powder, and vegetable stock to the saucepan. Bring to a boil and cook, covered, for 15 to 20 minutes or until all the vegetables are tender, stirring occasionally. Let cool slightly.

Transfer all the ingredients into a blender. Add the coconut milk and purée until you reach your desired consistency.

TIP The key ingredient in most curry spice blends? Turmeric! Golden, peppery, and warm, turmeric and its main active component curcumin offer numerous health benefits. As a potent anti-inflammatory, turmeric assists in reducing pain and disease in every system of the body, including the digestive system, heart, lungs, and brain.

High in protein and omega-3 fatty acids, fish is a great food to add to a baby's diet at any age and can even be puréed with first foods. This purée was inspired by the fish stews eaten along the Mediterranean Sea. A fragrant but simple stew of simmered carrots, red bell peppers, potato, and white fish seasoned with paprika, coriander, cumin, and cilantro, this purée offers a flavorful way to introduce your baby to the wonderful world of fish.

Spiced Fish Purée

WITH RED BELL PEPPERS + PAPRIKA

9+ MONTHS

MAKES 20 ounces
PREP TIME: 10 minutes
COOK TIME: 20 minutes

STORAGE
Refrigerator: 3 days
Freezer: 2 months

1 teaspoon olive oil

¼ onion, diced

2 carrots, peeled and chopped

2 red bell peppers, seeded and chopped

½ russet or sweet potato, peeled and chopped

½ pound white fish, such as cod, tilapia, or sole, cubed

1 tablespoon tomato paste

½ teaspoon sweet paprika

½ teaspoon ground coriander

½ teaspoon ground cumin

½ teaspoon dried cilantro

2 cups unsalted vegetable stock or water

In a medium saucepan, heat olive oil over medium heat. Add onion and sauté until tender, 5 minutes.

Add the carrots, red peppers, potato, fish, tomato paste, paprika, coriander, cumin, cilantro, and stock, and bring to a boil.

Reduce heat to low, and simmer for 20 minutes, stirring occasionally. Let cool slightly.

Place all the ingredients in a blender, and purée until you reach your desired consistency.

TIP Babies need a lot of omega-3 fatty acids for their brain, eye, and nerve development. Often, when babies start reducing their intake of breast milk in favor of solid foods, they no longer receive enough of this important nutrient. Fish provides a great source of omega-3 fatty acids, especially cold-water fatty fish like halibut, mackerel, and herring.

I made this rich green purée for my friend's baby who was suffering from a minor bout of iron deficiency. A baby's body absorbs iron best from food naturally loaded with iron—beef, clams, liver, spinach, sunflower seeds, and nuts. Here beef and spinach are puréed with vitamin C–filled broccoli, which helps the body absorb the iron. Beef, spinach, and broccoli are a bit intense for a baby's taste buds, so I add an apple for sweetening, plus leeks for smoothness. All combined, this purée not only tastes like a beef feast but also heals your baby from the inside out.

Pump Some Iron Beef Purée

9+ MONTHS

MAKES 20 ounces
PREP TIME: 10 minutes
COOK TIME: 20 minutes

STORAGE
Refrigerator: 3 days
Freezer: 2 months

½ pound beef, cubed

1 cup broccoli florets

2 leeks, white and green parts only, chopped

1 apple, cored and chopped

1 cup trimmed and roughly chopped packed spinach

½ cup water (reserved from steaming) or unsalted beef stock

Fill a medium saucepan with about 2 inches of water. Heat on medium until the water begins to boil.

Place the beef in a steamer basket over the boiling water, and cover for 10 minutes. Add the broccoli, leeks, apple, and spinach to the steamer basket, and cook for an additional 5 to 10 minutes or until all vegetables are tender and the beef is cooked through. Let cool slightly.

Place all of the ingredients in a blender or food processor, reserve steamed water, if using, and purée, adding liquid in ¼ cup increments, until you reach your desired consistency.

TIP Beef from grass-fed cows is rich in "heme" iron, the type most easily absorbed and used by your baby's body.

Finger Foods, Snacks, and Smoothies

(9+ MONTHS)

Frequently Asked Questions

My little one has only a couple of teeth. Will she choke if I give her chunks of food?

Babies' gums are surprisingly strong and tough! Most babies can gum their foods quite well even if they only have a tooth or two. Age-appropriate foods include a combination of chunkier purées that your baby can feed to herself with a spoon and small, soft pieces of cooked foods she can pick up with her fingers. Be sure the pieces of food you offer are soft and pliable, and go slowly, giving her pieces that take more time.

Let your baby gum each piece for a minute or two, especially when trying new textures, foods, or sizes of foods. Allowing babies to practice the act of chewing—even before they have a full mouth of teeth—is great for their development and actually helps them digest their food better.

Will using whole-fat milk and dairy products make my toddler fat?

No. Earlier in the book, I noted briefly that you should not avoid feeding your baby full-fat foods. Here's why: Healthy fats are a necessary structural component of the brain and central nervous system, which are developing very rapidly in your toddler. It's important to think about feeding your toddler the "right kind" of fat, especially when it comes to milk and dairy products. Milk in its most natural state is a full-fat food. It must be altered to reduce or remove its fat content, and this process unbalances the micronutrient ratio; specifically, it increases the overall percentage of carbohydrates—or sugars—in milk known as lactose. You lose the good fat in exchange for upping the sugar intake.

Low-fat foods were once considered to be a healthy choice to help people reduce calorie intake. But reduced-fat foods and drinks are not as filling, so toddlers and children may end up eating or drinking more milk or other calorie-laden foods.

Is it better for my toddler to graze throughout the day or have set mealtimes?

Reality happens, but try to schedule meals and snacks for your toddler similar to those of the rest of the family. In general, a combination of structured meals and semi-regular snack times provide enough routine for parents, plus flexibility for the little one whose hunger level may rise and fall throughout the day.

I'm in favor of regular meals and structured snacks so that at mealtime children can be hungry but not starved. Having a sense of both hunger and fullness is an intuitive component to how we develop and nurture our relationship with food from a young age. Losing that attunement to our bodies as we grow up is sometimes why adults don't recognize signals for feeling full or even an illness coming on.

What are some ways I can make sure my toddler has healthy snacks when we are on the go?

Toddler snacks are always on the go, right? Going on the floor, going out the car window, going in the dog's mouth! But whether or not the snacks end up in your toddler's mouth or smushed on her sister's head, you don't need a store-bought package or pouch to ensure snack portability.

Sometimes the best snacks take the least amount of work (thank you, Whole Foods), such as:

- Fresh-cut, bite-size soft fruits and vegetables

- Small cubes of mild, organic white Cheddar cheese. (Remember that string cheese products might have undergone processing, so your best bet is to cut cubes from a block of white Cheddar, which hasn't had any color added.)

- Wedges cut from whole-wheat pitas, or mini pitas for extra adorability

- With just a tad more work, you can prepare a smoothie.

- Homemade mini muffins require some planning ahead, but if you introduce me to a toddler who doesn't like mini muffins, I'll introduce you to my pet giraffe. Although toddlers will scarf a store-bought mini muffin just as heartily as a homemade one, when you make them at home, you can make sure you've got the killer combination of healthy and scrumptious.

My good friend Mary is one of those moms who somehow finds the time to be endlessly active, involved in more mommy groups than days of the week. She also has a vegetable garden to kill for *and* she knows how to cook. I should hate her, but every time our children have a play date, I get beyond excited to see what delicious snacks she's going to bring—and share! When Mary whipped out this mini Italian caprese—with tomato and basil from her garden, no less—our girls went wild for it. *Buon appetito!*

Bambino Caprese

9+ MONTHS

MAKES 1 cup
PREP TIME: 5 minutes

STORAGE
Refrigerator: 2 days
Freezer: Not recommended

¼ cup mini mozzarella balls, liquid drained and cut in half

3 tablespoons pitted and sliced black olives

10 cherry tomatoes, cut in half

3 basil leaves, thinly sliced

Place the mozzarella, olives, and tomatoes between 2 pieces of paper towels, and blot away any excess moisture.

Add all ingredients into a small container and toss lightly.

TIP Is your baby wakeful? (Do YOU need more sleep? Is that even a fair question for parents with young ones?) Basil contains chemicals that reduce tension and promote sleep in a baby. You read that right: eating basil = extra sleep!

When beets are gently roasted or steamed, they turn into a sugary, candy-like treat that my Ellie never passes up. Because this salad is made with soft beets and oranges, it is perfect for toddlers and babies just starting to use their pincer-like fingers.

Sunshine Finger Salad + Golden Beets + Oranges

9+ MONTHS

MAKES 1 cup
PREP TIME: 5 minutes

STORAGE
Refrigerator: 2 days

1 golden beet, cooked, peeled and chopped

1 orange, peeled, seeded, segmented, and chopped (canned mandarin oranges, without sugar or artificial sweetener, also work well)

2 mint leaves, finely chopped

Place all the ingredients into a small bowl and gently toss.

．．．．．．．．．．．．．．．．．．．．．．．．．．

TIP While this recipe calls for golden beets, feel free to use red, radish, baby, or any beet variety you find. Since red beets can be a tad messy, I find that after you cook and chop them, it helps to put them into a colander and rinse under cold water until the water runs clean.

．．．．．．．．．．．．．．．．．．．．．．．．．．

Magic is what happens when you make this recipe—pink magic to be exact. Apples and beets simmered to perfection with cinnamon, cloves, and a dash of ginger all come together to create pink magic applesauce that all toddlers, princesses, and mamas love to eat. No magic wand required.

Pink Applesauce

9+ MONTHS

MAKES 3 cups
PREP TIME: 10 minutes
COOK TIME: 45 minutes

STORAGE
Refrigerator: 2 weeks

6 apples, peeled, cored, and chopped

¼ small red beet, finely chopped

1 teaspoon ground cinnamon

¼ teaspoon ground cloves

⅛ teaspoon ground nutmeg

Pinch ground ginger

½ cup water

Place all the ingredients in a medium saucepan and heat on low-to-medium heat, covered, for 30 to 45 minutes, stirring occasionally. Let cool slightly before serving.

For a chunky applesauce, smash the apple and beet mixture with the back of a wooden spoon. For a smooth applesauce, transfer all the ingredients to a blender or food processor, add water, and purée until you reach your desired consistency.

TIP This recipe is great for an on-the-go snack for your toddler. Simply put applesauce into a reusable pouch, seal, and take along on your kiddo's next adventure.

I haven't met a toddler who can resist plump, juicy blueberries and sweet grapes. When combined with a citrus splash of freshly squeezed orange juice, this purple snack filled with calcium, vitamin C, potassium, and powerful anti-oxidants will be gone in seconds. Whole grapes can be a choking hazard for kids up to the age of two, so make sure to slice each grape in half or quarters.

Purple Pick-Up Salad
WITH GRAPES + BLUEBERRIES
9+ MONTHS

MAKES 1 cup
PREP TIME: 5 minutes

STORAGE
Refrigerator: 2 days

½ cup purple grapes, cut in half

½ cup blueberries

1 tablespoon freshly squeezed
    orange juice

Place grapes and blueberries in small bowl, mix gently with orange juice, and serve immediately.

TIP For a healthy mom's snack, top a cup of Greek yogurt with the grape mixture, and add a sprinkle of homemade granola. I find the juice from this salad is enough to sweeten the yogurt, but feel free to add a tablespoon of honey if you like.

At a recent play date, my good friend Jen pulled out a tub of cream cheese and crackers and declared her contribution to snack time a complete failure. I, on the other hand, pronounced it pure genius! While this spread is mixed with a heaping portion of spinach, leaks, and parsley, its creamy goodness is what keeps the toddlers coming back for more. And isn't watching the little ones run back for seconds or even thirds every parent's dream?

Green Dream Cream Cheese Spread

12+ MONTHS

MAKES 1½ cups
PREP TIME: 5 minutes
CHILL TIME: 30 minutes

STORAGE
Refrigerator: 1 week

1 leek, trimmed and roughly chopped from the light green and white part of the stalk

1 cup baby spinach

1 tablespoon roughly chopped fresh parsley

½ garlic clove

1 (8-ounce) block cream cheese

Place all the ingredients into a food processor.

Blend until fully mixed and the consistency is smooth, scraping down the sides every 30 seconds.

Scrape or spoon the cheese spread into a small airtight container, and place it in the refrigerator.

Let the spread harden for 30 minutes before serving.

TIP Serve with crackers, with veggie sticks, on sandwiches, in scrambled eggs, or even on top of a baked potato.

I first made these mini muffins for a group of toddlers, and, in a matter of minutes, they had completely disappeared (the muffins, that is—it took the kids a few extra moments to scatter). Everyone needs a good kid-friendly muffin up their sleeve, so this one is going to be yours. A warm and spicy muffin featuring both a vegetable and a fruit, low on processed sugar, and packed with protein, this muffin is a great staple for your entire family.

Carrot + Apple Spice Mini Muffins

12+ MONTHS

MAKES 36 mini muffins
PREP TIME: 15 minutes
COOK TIME: 20 minutes

STORAGE
Airtight container: 3 days

Cooking spray or muffin liners

1 cup whole-wheat flour

1 cup all-purpose white flour

1 teaspoon baking powder

1 teaspoon baking soda

½ teaspoon salt

2 tablespoons ground cinnamon

½ teaspoon ground nutmeg

½ teaspoon ground cloves

½ cup firmly packed dark brown sugar

2 large eggs

½ cup applesauce

½ cup plain yogurt

4 tablespoons butter, melted

1 cup grated apple (roughly 1 apple)

1 cup grated carrot (roughly 2 carrots)

½ cup chopped walnuts (optional)

¼ cup firmly packed dark brown sugar

1 teaspoon ground cinnamon

Preheat the oven to 350°F. Spray a mini muffin pan with cooking spray, or line with paper liners.

In a medium bowl, stir together the flours, baking powder, baking soda, salt, cinnamon, nutmeg, and cloves. Set aside.

In a large bowl, whisk the eggs, applesauce, and yogurt together. Stir in the butter. Pour into the flour mixture, and gently stir until just incorporated.

Add the apple, carrot, and walnuts, and stir until just combined. The batter will be very thick.

Spoon the batter evenly into the prepared muffin pan.

For the topping, mix together the brown sugar and cinnamon, and sprinkle it onto the tops of all of the muffins.

Bake for 15 to 20 minutes or until a toothpick can be inserted into the center of a muffin and comes out clean.

Let the muffins cool in the pan for 5 minutes, then transfer them to a wire rack and let them cool completely.

....

TIP These mini muffins are easy to pack and make a perfect snack for preschool, day care, or a toddler on the go. If your kiddo goes to a nut-free preschool or day care, make sure to leave out the walnuts.

....

When your little one is coming down with a case of the "yuckies," turn to this smoothie. Filled with oranges, cherries, carrots, and a little honey, this tasty smoothie will not only soothe sore throats, but with over 90 milligrams of vitamin C, it will also kick those nasties to the curb in no time.

Vitamin C–Kick Smoothie

12+ MONTHS

MAKES 1 toddler and 1 adult serving
PREP TIME: 5 minutes

STORAGE
Serve immediately

2 oranges, peeled and cut into quarters

½ cup pitted and frozen cherries

¼ cup shredded carrots

1 cup freshly squeezed orange juice

½ cup plain yogurt

2 tablespoons honey

1 cup ice

Place all ingredients into a blender, and blend until smooth.

Pour into 2 glasses and enjoy.

TIP Raw honey is different from regular honey you might find at the grocery store. Since it hasn't been pasteurized, heated, or processed in any way, raw honey contains many valuable health benefits. Full of minerals, vitamins, enzymes, and powerful antioxidants, raw honey also has anti-bacterial, anti-viral, and antifungal properties. Consuming raw honey on a regular basis may help strengthen the immune system and even prevent seasonal allergies. However, DO NOT GIVE HONEY TO A BABY UNDER 12 MONTHS.

Let's be honest, it is so easy to buy a box of organic Cheddar bunnies, pour some out for your kid, and call snack time done. I've been guilty of this myself on numerous occasions. When I was pregnant with my second child, this snack-time habit was becoming the norm around my house, so I went to the kitchen and got to work making a better-tasting, more nutritious Cheddar cracker. With minimal time and energy, you can make these savory, melt-in-your-mouth crackers that contain only seven ingredients—all of which you can pronounce.

Savory Cheddar Crackers + Rosemary

12+ MONTHS

MAKES 3 cups
PREP TIME: 25 minutes
COOK TIME: 15 minutes

STORAGE
Airtight container: 5 days

Cooking spray

6 ounces white Cheddar cheese, shredded

¼ cup butter, cut into pieces

¾ cup whole-wheat flour

1 teaspoon salt

½ teaspoon garlic powder

1 teaspoon finely chopped fresh rosemary

1 tablespoon milk

Preheat the oven to 350°F. Spray a baking sheet with cooking spray.

Place the cheese, butter, flour, salt, garlic powder, and rosemary into a food processor, and pulse until the ingredients turn into coarse crumbs.

Add the milk, and continue pulsing until a dough ball forms.

On a wooden surface, place the dough ball and break into 4 smaller balls. Roll each ball into a long rope approximately ½-inch thick. Wrap each rope with plastic wrap, and place in the freezer for 10 to 15 minutes, or until hard but not frozen.

Take out 1 rope at a time, and place it back onto the cutting board. Cut ⅛-inch-thick slices off the rope, and place on the baking sheet. Leave some room around each cracker as they will spread a little.

Poke a small hole in the middle of each cracker, and bake for 12 to 15 minutes, or until the crackers are just starting to turn golden brown.

On a wire rack, let them cool completely.

TIP This recipe is for a savory Cheddar cracker, which both Ellie and my husband devoured. For a more true-to-form goldfish cracker, omit the rosemary, but stick with white Cheddar, as the yellow color of Cheddar is added, not natural. You can also roll this dough out, and cut with any cute animal or fish cookie cutter you have on hand.

Mom and I had a little competition this winter over whose homemade hot cocoa reigned supreme, complete with tasting cups, dunking treats, and a steep prize—a gorgeous hot chocolate pot from Williams-Sonoma. The verdict: we both won, because anytime you drink homemade hot cocoa, you can't lose. This recipe offers a hot cocoa base that combines both of our recipes. Consider it a not-quite-blank canvas. Your hot cocoa can achieve edible masterpiece status with any of the eight add-ins suggested. Ain't got nothing but love for this versatile recipe.

8 Days a Week Hot Cocoa

12+ MONTHS

MAKES 8 toddler servings
PREP TIME: 5 minutes
COOK TIME: 10 minutes

STORAGE
Airtight container: Hot cocoa base can store for 2 months

FOR THE HOT COCOA BASE

¼ cup finely chopped semi-sweet or dark chocolate

4 teaspoons dark cocoa powder

¼ cup sugar

½ teaspoon sea salt

FOR THE HOT COCOA

1 cup milk of your choice

1 heaping tablespoon of hot cocoa base

In an airtight container, mix together chocolate, cocoa powder, sugar, and salt.

In a small saucepan, heat the milk, cocoa mixture, and any other add-ins you want (see next page) over medium heat for 10 minutes, whisking until all the chocolate is melted.

Serve and enjoy immediately.

TIP Dark chocolate has more antioxidant activity, polyphenols, and flavanols than even super fruits like blueberries and acai berries. Cheers to that!

ADD-INS

ORANGE COCOA: Add 1 teaspoon of grated orange zest to the mix before pouring.

MEXICAN COCOA: Add a pinch of cayenne and nutmeg while mixing.

PUMPKIN SPICE: Add 1 teaspoon maple syrup and ½ teaspoon pumpkin pie spice while mixing.

NUTELLA: Add 1 tablespoon Nutella while mixing.

COCONUT: Use coconut milk while making the cocoa, and add a sprinkle of toasted coconut to top.

PEANUT BUTTER: Add 1 tablespoon of creamy peanut butter while mixing, and serve with pretzels for dunking.

ALMOND: Add ½ teaspoon almond extract and a pinch of nutmeg while mixing.

MAMA'S COCOA: Add 2 ounces peppermint schnapps into a mug, and add hot cocoa over the schnapps.

When I was pregnant with Parker, my second child, I ate this wrap almost every day, which means my toddler Ellie did, too—good thing she loves it! Easy, portable, and completely flexible regarding choice and amount of fillings, this wrap can easily become your go-to snack or lunch recipe . . . whether you are pregnant or not.

Hummus + Feta + Carrot Wrap

12+ MONTHS

MAKES 1 toddler and 1 adult serving
PREP TIME: 5 minutes

STORAGE
Refrigerator: 1 day

2 (10-inch) whole-wheat tortillas

½ cup Pucker-Up Lemon Hummus
(page 111), or flavor of choice

½ cup shredded carrots

½ cup trimmed and roughly chopped
spinach (optional for toddler)

¼ cup feta, crumbled

¼ teaspoon red pepper flakes (optional
for toddler)

Lay out both of the tortillas, and spread half of the hummus on each one, leaving a 1-inch border of tortilla clean around the edge.

Place the carrots, spinach, and feta down the center of each tortilla. Sprinkle red pepper flakes on top.

Roll each tortilla as tightly as you can. Cut into 5 (2-inch) sections.

TIP Wraps are a great, portable way for your toddler to take in some healthy greens, protein, and vegetables. I like to make smaller slices, or pinwheels, out of the wraps, so the little ones can handle them without a struggle.

We eat a lot of apple slices for snack time in my house. It can get boring—really boring. I concocted this dip after I stood in front of my pantry for a full ten minutes, determined not to eat another ho-hum apple. Made with ingredients I always have on hand, this dip offered a fun, new way to liven up our snack time and has become our new go-to favorite. Slightly warm, this apple dip is a perfect combination of creamy and crunchy, salty and sweet, simple and flavorful.

Warm Honey + Goat Cheese Apple Dip

12+ MONTHS

MAKES 3 toddler servings
PREP TIME: 5 minutes

STORAGE
Serve immediately

4 tablespoons goat cheese

2 tablespoons honey

1 tablespoon finely chopped walnuts

1 apple (Granny Smith or Honeycrisp),
   cored and sliced

Place the goat cheese in a small bowl, and heat in the microwave for 10 to 15 seconds or until just warm and creamy.

Add the honey and walnuts, and stir until well combined.

Serve with apple slices.

TIP Since apples are the number-one food on the Dirty Dozen list, I suggest using organic apples for this recipe.

Tea time at our house involves a yellow duck, a paint-splattered pink rabbit, purple tea cups, magnetic alphabet letters, a colander, and of course a three-tiered tower for finger sandwiches. Real sandwiches are a must, because in my opinion eating pretend play food is no fun. And while I am still asking "Why a colander?" I do know our tea ceremony will always include these finger sandwiches.

Curried Egg Finger Sandwiches + Mango Chutney

12+ MONTHS

MAKES 8 small finger servings
PREP TIME: 10 minutes

STORAGE
Serve immediately

4 hard-boiled eggs, chopped

3 tablespoons plain Greek yogurt

1 tablespoon mayonnaise

1 teaspoon orange juice

½ teaspoon curry powder

Salt

Freshly ground black pepper

2 tablespoons mango chutney

4 slices thin whole-wheat bread

In a medium bowl, add the eggs, Greek yogurt, mayonnaise, orange juice, and curry powder. Mix gently and season with the salt and pepper.

Spread the mango chutney over 2 slices of bread and then top with the egg salad. Top with remaining slices of bread, pressing lightly. Trim off the crusts with a serrated knife, then cut along both diagonals to form 4 triangles.

TIP No hard-boiled eggs on hand? Get cooking. In a medium saucepan, add the eggs and cover them with an inch of water. Over high heat, bring water to a rapid boil. Then remove the pan from the heat, cover, and let sit for 12 minutes. Using a slotted spoon, transfer the eggs to a bowl of ice water. Let the eggs sit in the ice water for at least 3 minutes or until cool enough to handle. Peel, chop, and enjoy.

This recipe begins with a mouthwatering aroma and ends with a big BANG! One day the thought of warm, spiced almond butter became too much to resist. I was nervous to make my own, but once the smell of warm maple syrup and almonds started drifting from my oven, I knew I had made the right decision. After a quick roast and lots of noise from the food processor, this butter makes a simple and tasty treat for your toddler.

Roasted Maple-Spiced Almond Butter

12+ MONTHS

MAKES 2 cups
PREP TIME: 20 minutes
COOK TIME: 15 minutes

STORAGE
Refrigerator: 2 months

2 cups raw almonds

2 tablespoons maple syrup

½ teaspoon ground cinnamon

⅛ teaspoon ground ginger

¼ teaspoon vanilla extract

2 teaspoons coconut oil

Pinch sea salt

Preheat the oven to 325°F. Line a baking sheet with foil or parchment paper.

On the baking sheet, combine the almonds and maple syrup until all of the almonds are well coated and in a single layer.

Bake for 15 minutes, stirring once halfway through baking time. Let cool for 10 minutes.

Pour the almonds into a food processor, and pulse in 2-second bursts for 30 seconds (this will be very loud) to start breaking down the almonds.

Add the cinnamon, ginger, vanilla, coconut oil, and salt, and continue to process on full speed for 10 to 15 minutes, or until your almonds are completely smooth.

TIP You can serve this almond butter as a dip for apples or bananas, smeared on top of a thick piece of toast for a traditional sandwich, spooned into plain oatmeal, or as a base for an almond maple smoothie.

My daughter's first food obsession began when she was one—with blueberries! During that magical summer, she consumed pint after pint, which lovingly made us refer to her as Violet Beauregarde from *Willy Wonka and the Chocolate Factory*. So when winter rolled around, and blueberries were no longer readily available, I turned to frozen ones. After many attempts to find just the right blueberry smoothie, this was the golden ticket. This smoothie delivers a bold blueberry flavor (and color) with a good serving of protein, omega-3s, and greens to keep your little one rolling along.

Blueberry Blast-Off Smoothie

12+ MONTHS

MAKES 1 toddler and 1 adult serving
PREP TIME: 5 minutes

STORAGE
Serve immediately

1½ cups blueberries, frozen

1 banana, peeled

½ cup plain Greek yogurt

1 small handful spinach

1 tablespoon honey

2 teaspoons flaxseeds

¼ teaspoon nutmeg

½ cup ice

½ cup milk of choice, divided

Place all the ingredients into a blender and purée until smooth. Add additional milk, ¼ cup at a time, until you reach your desired consistency.

Pour into 2 glasses and enjoy.

TIP Flaxseeds are a powerhouse of nutrition for your baby—so include them in smoothies or oatmeal, or sprinkle them onto finger salads. They contain omega-3 fatty acids called "alpha-linolenic acid" (or ALA) that protect against cardiovascular disease, inflammation, and neuromuscular disease. In addition, flaxseeds contain lignans and fiber to benefit a baby's digestive system.

I bribe my toddler. It's true. I bribe her at the store, at the park, or even sometimes at home when I need my iPad back. The treat I offer to end tantrums, ensure smooth errands, and get a little peace and quiet is this smoothie. Made with rich coconut and chocolate, this smoothie could be called dessert except that it's filled with protein, fiber, calcium, and omega-3s from the yogurt, almond butter, and flaxseeds, which makes it perfect for an anytime bribe—er, treat.

Almond Joy Smoothie

12+ MONTHS

MAKES 1 toddler and 1 adult serving
PREP TIME: 5 minutes

STORAGE
Serve immediately

1 banana, peeled

½ cup plain Greek yogurt

¼ cup shredded coconut, plus sprinkle
    for top

1½ tablespoons cocoa powder

1 tablespoon peanut or almond butter

1 teaspoon flaxseeds

2 dates, pitted and roughly chopped

1 cup coconut milk

1 cup ice

1 teaspoon carob or dark chocolate chips

Place banana, Greek yogurt, coconut, cocoa powder, peanut butter, flaxseeds, dates, coconut milk, and ice into a blender, and blend until smooth. Add carob chips and pulse 5 to 10 times or until the carob chips are chopped into small pieces.

Pour into 2 glasses, and top with a sprinkle of coconut.

TIP One of the healthiest natural sweeteners, dates are loaded with nutrients including iron for the blood, fiber for the digestive tract, vitamin A for the eyes, and potassium for the heart. Dates have historically been eaten for their therapeutic properties, and in fact, many home remedies for inducing sleep include a stewed date in warm milk.

This hummus is HumMAZING—yes, I went there! Quite simply, it will bring your store-bought hummus days to an end. Creamy and smooth, this hummus recipe with a citrus twist includes just enough lemon zest to bring out a little pucker face on your toddler.

Pucker-Up Lemon Hummus

12+ MONTHS

MAKES 1½ cups
PREP TIME: 10 minutes

STORAGE
Refrigerator: 1 week

1 can chickpeas, drained and washed

¼ cup lemon juice, fresh squeezed, about 1 lemon

½ teaspoon lemon peel, zested

1 tablespoon olive oil

1 garlic clove, minced

⅓ cup tahini

½ teaspoon paprika

½ teaspoon mild yellow curry powder

¼ teaspoon salt

Place all of the ingredients into a food processor, and purée until smooth.

Taste and adjust seasoning, if needed.

My husband's family has been known to make 1,307-mile milkshake drop-offs. Let's just say they take their milkshakes very seriously—a legacy my husband is working very hard to pass down to our daughter. So I knew my critics would be tough on this "milkshake" recipe, but they both dug in and didn't stop until their straws had slurped up every ounce of goodness. They even asked for seconds. This healthy banana "milkshake" really passed the test!

Bumpin' Banana "Milkshake"

12+ MONTHS

MAKES 1 toddler and 1 adult serving
PREP TIME: 5 minutes

STORAGE
Serve immediately

1 large ripe banana, peeled and quartered

1 cup whole milk

½ cup Greek yogurt

1 cup ice

2 teaspoons honey

1 teaspoon vanilla extract

½ teaspoon ground cinnamon

¼ teaspoon ground nutmeg

Place all the ingredients into a blender, and blend until smooth.

Pour into 2 glasses and enjoy.

TIP Not sure what to do with those brown bananas? Freeze them! Frozen bananas are great for smoothies and "milkshakes." To freeze, simply peel, slice the banana in half, and place in a zipper lock bag. Store bag in the freezer for use when needed.

I started making these energy balls right after my youngest daughter, Parker, was born, because I needed a quick and healthy snack during all those late-night feedings. While my breastfeeding mind craved sugar, my post-baby body wanted something nutritious. This was a perfect solution. Made into small portions with healthy ingredients and no refined sugar, these energy balls hit the spot. Even better that they taste like Nutella—yep, you heard that right. No wonder my secret stash was soon invaded by my husband and toddler. Now I make these energy balls for our entire family—for hikes, family adventures, and of course my late-night feeding treats.

Double-Chocolate Energy Balls + Hazelnuts

12+ MONTHS

MAKES 25 (1-inch) balls
PREP TIME: 10 minutes (plus 2 hours chilling time)

STORAGE
Refrigerator: 1 week

1 cup dry old-fashioned oats

½ cup creamy peanut butter

½ cup ground flaxseed

½ cup raw honey

3 tablespoons dark cocoa powder

½ cup finely chopped hazelnuts

½ cup dark chocolate chips

2 teaspoons vanilla extract

In a medium bowl, stir the oats, peanut butter, flaxseeds, honey, cocoa powder, hazelnuts, chocolate chips, and vanilla extract together until well combined. This mixture will be thick, and I find it is easier to combine with my own hands.

Roll the mixture into 1-inch balls, roughly 1 tablespoon, and place them on a baking sheet. If the mixture is being difficult, you can place the bowl in the fridge for 10 to 15 minutes to harden up.

Place the baking sheet in the fridge, and let chill for 1 to 2 hours until the balls harden.

Transfer to an airtight container, and keep stored in the refrigerator.

Loaded with tart dried cherries, crunchy pistachios, and sweet dark chocolate, these chewy granola bars are a perfect snack—for both of you. These granola bars push the limits with an almost 50/50 ratio of extras versus oats. After more than a dozen tries, I found just the right "glue" to hold it all together: honey, maple syrup, and applesauce. Flawlessly chewy and chunky—the Perfect Granola Bar.

Perfect Chunky + Chewy Granola Bar

12+ MONTHS

MAKES 20 big bars
PREP TIME: 10 minutes
COOK TIME: 45 minutes

STORAGE
Airtight container: 1 week

Cooking spray

¾ cup pistachios

2½ cups rolled oats

¾ cup whole-wheat flour

¾ cup dried cherries

¾ cup dark chocolate chips or chunks

¼ cup packed dark brown sugar

1 teaspoon ground cinnamon

1 teaspoon sea salt

¼ cup honey

¼ cup maple syrup

¼ cup applesauce

½ cup coconut oil, melted

1 egg, beaten

Preheat the oven to 350°F. Generously spray a 9-by-13-inch baking pan with cooking spray.

On another baking sheet, scatter the pistachios and bake for 10 to 15 minutes until fragrant and golden brown, stirring halfway through baking time. Let cool slightly.

In a large bowl, mix together the oats, flour, dried cherries, pistachios, chocolate chips, brown sugar, cinnamon, and sea salt.

Add in the honey, maple syrup, applesauce, coconut oil, and egg, and mix until all ingredients are well incorporated.

Pour the oat mixture into the baking pan, and pat down the mixture with the back of a spoon or your hand until firmly and evenly spread.

Bake for 25 to 30 minutes, or until the bars begin to turn a golden brown. Cool for 15 minutes in the pan, then cut into bars while still somewhat warm. Once cut, let the bars cool completely.

You can serve immediately, but they tend to be even better the next day.

Smoothie time is game time in our house! As soon as the blender comes out, the smoothie making game begins. It goes like this: Ellie picks an ingredient, then I pick an ingredient, and we repeat until the counter is full—or the fridge is empty. The game either creates major winners or total flops, but the smoothie I offer to you here is a real winner! Combining pineapple, banana, and coconut for delicious tropical flavor, with spinach, Greek yogurt, and chia seeds for a healthy base, this smoothie is an all-star drink.

Healthy Tropical Green Smoothie

12+ MONTHS

MAKES: 1 toddler and 1 adult serving
PREP TIME: 5 minutes

STORAGE
Serve immediately

1 cup pineapple, fresh or frozen

2 cups loosely packed spinach

1 medium banana, ripe and peeled

3 tablespoons shredded coconut

½ cup plain Greek yogurt

1 cup milk of your choice

½ teaspoon chia seeds

1½ cups ice

Place all the ingredients into a blender, and pureé until smooth.

Pour into 2 glasses and enjoy.

TIP Popeye was on to something! The list of nutritional compounds in spinach is truly impressive, including iron, carotenoids, antioxidants, vitamin K, coenzyme Q10, B vitamins, minerals, chlorophyll, polyphenols, betaine, and even omega-3 fatty acids. All these nutrients work together to promote your toddler's best health.

This tempting bread has just the right amount of sweetness. Filled with plump juicy blueberries and healthy zucchini—that's right, this bread contains both a fruit and a vegetable! The truth is you don't even notice the zucchini, but it keeps the bread super moist, making it perfect for breakfast or snack time.

Zucchini + Blueberry Bread

12+ MONTHS

MAKES 10 to 12 slices
PREP TIME: 10 minutes
COOK TIME: 60 minutes

STORAGE
Airtight container: 5 days

Cooking spray

1½ cups whole-wheat flour

½ teaspoon salt

½ teaspoon baking soda

½ teaspoon baking powder

1 teaspoon ground cinnamon

¼ teaspoon nutmeg

¼ teaspoon cloves

1 egg

⅓ cup coconut oil, melted

⅓ cup unsweetened applesauce, homemade or store bought

¼ cup plain yogurt

½ cup sugar

2 teaspoons vanilla extract

1 cup zucchini, grated

1 cup blueberries, fresh or frozen

Preheat the oven to 325°F. Generously spray an 8-inch loaf pan with cooking spray.

In a medium bowl, mix together the flour, salt, baking soda, baking powder, cinnamon, nutmeg, and cloves.

In a large bowl, whisk together the egg, coconut oil, applesauce, yogurt, sugar, and vanilla.

Add the flour mixture to the wet mixture and stir until just combined. Fold in the zucchini and the blueberries until just combined.

Spoon the batter into the loaf pan and bake for 50 to 60 minutes, or until golden brown and a toothpick inserted into the center of the loaf comes out clean.

Let the loaf cool in the pan for 25 minutes, then remove it from the pan, and let it completely cool on a wire rack.

I crafted this granola for my little Ellie with some of her favorite ingredients—blueberries, coconut flakes, and almonds—and a few healthy additions: flaxseeds, coconut oil, and a pinch of Himalayan sea salt. Sprinkle this granola over Greek yogurt mixed with fresh fruit, pair it with organic whole milk, or take it along as an on-the-go snack. However you devour it, consider doubling or tripling the recipe. You won't regret it.

Ellie's Favorite Granola

12+ MONTHS

MAKES 4 cups
PREP TIME: 10 minutes
COOK TIME: 45 minutes

STORAGE
Airtight container: 3 months

Cooking spray

2 cups old-fashioned rolled oats

½ cup shredded coconut

1½ cups sliced or slivered almonds

¼ cup flaxseeds

¼ cup coconut oil, melted

¼ cup honey

1 teaspoon ground cinnamon

½ teaspoon vanilla extract

½ teaspoon salt, Himalayan or sea salt

1 cup dried blueberries

TIP Many parents hesitate to add salt to their baby's or toddler's food. While it is true that refined and bleached table salt isn't a good idea for your baby, beautiful pink Himalayan sea salt is. Packed with 84 essential minerals, this salt aids proper digestion and boosts the immune system.

Heat the oven to 300°F.

Generously spray the baking sheet with cooking spray.

In a large bowl, combine the oats, coconut, almonds, flaxseeds, coconut oil, honey, cinnamon, vanilla extract, and salt. Mix until all of the ingredients are well combined.

Spread the oat mixture onto the baking sheet in an even layer.

Bake for 35 to 45 minutes, stirring the granola and rotating the baking sheet in the oven every 15 minutes, or until the oats are golden brown. For a chunkier granola, do not stir the granola after you take it out of the oven, but let it completely cool on the baking sheet. If you prefer a looser granola, take the granola out of the oven, immediately stir well, then let it cool on the baking sheet.

Once the granola has completely cooled, toss well with the dried blueberries.

Our Meal Is Your Meal

(12+ MONTHS)

Frequently Asked Questions

My child is one year old and is, well, a bit more discerning about food. How can I make sure that veggies get eaten?

Although it's tempting, we really shouldn't try to get our children to eat more vegetables in any of the sneaky ways often advertised in parenting magazines or commercials. Boosting nutritional content of any recipe is a great idea, but try first to make healthy foods fun in and of themselves. Try telling your little one that broccoli looks like little trees. You might not be enticed by the idea of eating a tree, but one of the best things about our kids is that they don't have the same hang-ups we do. (Why does my daughter adore spiders and snails?) As children grow, the "first" game—"Who can eat x first?"—is especially useful in getting them to eat a food that isn't immediately appealing. Older toddlers *always* want to be first and will likely chow down on something that they don't love simply to beat you to it!

For better or worse, our children have free will in this process, not to mention unique taste buds! Some will naturally love veggies, others will not. Keep offering vegetables in a variety of healthy recipes—include both freshly cooked and raw—and let your child know that eating them is part of the plan for long-term healthy eating. Let your child see *you* munching on a fresh green salad, dipping crudités into a creamy hummus dip, and helping yourself to another serving of roasted cauliflower.

How much should my toddler be eating right now?

Here's the short answer: enough to satisfy their feelings of hunger. How often your toddler eats is still more important than how much, because you can control one but not the other.

One of the most useful signs that you can teach your preverbal little one is "all done." Once babies learn this sign, they use it quite effectively. But even if your child can sign, it doesn't mean you shouldn't talk about how her tummy feels, too. Encourage them to let you know with a nod when they are hungry ("like a dinosaur") and a head shake when they are full ("tummy is happy"). Trust their body to regulate these innate sensations. If they are pushing away their plate, turning their head to the side, saying "no," or giving you any impression that they are finished, you should receive that message loud and clear. Older toddlers (24+ months) still know their limits but can be quite savvy in using their vocabulary. With them, "all done" might simply mean they *want* to be all done. It's worth offering a few more bites with this more easily distracted age group.

Many of us grew up in the "clean plate club." But given what we know about toddler self-regulation, it's better to let your child determine the end of her mealtime. You still call the shots on what the meal includes, but now your toddler has a role in mealtime, too. Let your young child point to or say what she wants to eat from the larger ordering. You may find this approach can turn a picky eater into a food lover!

What other drinks beside water and milk can my toddler enjoy?

Water is the best choice for your toddler. Active all day long, playing, exploring, and learning, your child uses up a lot from her water stores, and her body needs sufficient hydration for proper nervous system functioning, digestive health, supple skin, and more. Milk functions really more like a food, with its macronutrient density and satiating calorie content. Think of it as part of her nutrition rather than hydration, and try to limit serving it to mealtimes or as part of a snack.

Fresh-pressed organic fruits and vegetable juices make wonderfully hydrating beverages for your child—you can make them at home or buy them at the health food store. Fresh juice contributes not only water, but loads of vitamins and minerals that help with electrolyte balance and energy.

Caffeine-free herbal teas, served weak and at room temperature or slightly warmed, make excellent hydrating tonics when your child has a cold or when it's cold outside. A favorite among children is Rooibos (also known as African Red Bush) tea. Naturally sweet and not at all bitter, Rooibos is also beneficial for the immune and digestive systems, and it can be a decidedly calming ritual to have an afternoon cup of tea with a healthy snack.

Salads are a tricky thing for toddlers. Ellie tries a piece of lettuce from time to time, but usually spits it back out with a perplexed look on her face. I get it; lettuce is boring and, quite frankly, has an odd texture. But who says you need greens in a salad? This finger salad offers chunky bites that your toddler can easily pick up and munch on, tossed in a tasty dressing full of good-for-you fat, and lime zest. It's a perfect side dish, quick lunch, or healthy snack on the go.

Edamame + Corn + Tomato
FINGER SALAD

12+ MONTHS

MAKES 4 small servings
PREP TIME: 5 minutes
COOK TIME: 5 minutes

STORAGE
Refrigerator: 1 day

2 tablespoons olive oil

1 teaspoon dried cilantro

½ lime, juiced

Salt

Freshly ground black pepper

2 cups edamame, shelled and frozen

1 cup corn kernels, frozen

12 cherry tomatoes, halved or quartered

In a medium bowl, whisk together the olive oil, cilantro, and lime, and season with salt and pepper to taste.

Bring a medium saucepan full of water to a boil, over high heat. Add the edamame and boil for 3 minutes. Add the corn and cook for an additional minute. Drain and rinse with cool water.

Add the cooked edamame, corn, and tomatoes to the bowl with the dressing and gently combine.

Cover and refrigerate for 1 to 2 hours so all the flavors can blend.

TIP Edamame is a star in the legume family! Just ½ cup of these little emerald green soy beans really boosts the fiber (9 grams!), vitamin, and mineral content of your baby's diet. More good news: soy beans are one of the few plant sources of complete protein.

I'm not sure what I expect from my pantry as I stand gazing into it every morning, as if it were restocked and refueled by a magical fairy during the night. In most cases, an amazing power snack for my toddler does not miraculously appear, and I'm tempted to settle for another container of dried raisins. But if I take about two more minutes (and two more ounces of energy), this healthy snack can be ready. Part crunch, part sweet, part chewy, this salad has it all—including those raisins, which of course get devoured first.

Carrot + Mango + Raisins

FINGER SALAD

12+ MONTHS

MAKES 4 small servings
PREP TIME: 5 minutes

STORAGE
Refrigerator: 1 day

1 tablespoon olive oil

1 teaspoon Dijon mustard

1 lime, juiced

1 tablespoon honey

Salt

Freshly ground black pepper

4 large carrots, peeled and shredded

1 mango, seeded, peeled, and cut into matchsticks

2 tablespoons raisins

In medium bowl, whisk together the olive oil, Dijon mustard, lime juice, and honey, and season with salt and pepper.

Add the carrots, mango, and raisins, and gently combine until all ingredients are well coated.

TIP I like to keep a large Mason jar filled with an emergency snack mixture of dried blueberries, dried cherries, dried cranberries, golden raisins, and raisins (all from the bulk section of my grocery store) in my pantry, so when I don't have those two extra minutes, I can pull out a more interesting fruit combo than just raisins.

I should call this recipe "Spa Salad for Toddlers"—before you roll your eyes, you know that the signature spa offering of citrus and cucumber water is the first sign that relaxation lies ahead. And in fact, I got the inspiration for this recipe from a delicious salad I ate during an all-day spa retreat. Of course, that was long before I had kids, and the relaxation of that day is a distant memory, but the flavors of the salad have endured: creamy avocado paired with crunchy cucumber and zesty orange, the perfect blend of foods that makes me relax from the inside out.

Orange + Avocado + Cucumber
FINGER SALAD

12+ MONTHS

MAKES 4 small servings
PREP TIME: 5 minutes

STORAGE
Serve immediately

1 tablespoon olive oil

2 teaspoons honey

2 teaspoons apple cider vinegar

Salt

1 avocado, semi-firm, diced

1 cucumber, seeded and diced

1 orange, peeled and chopped

In a medium bowl, whisk together the olive oil, honey, and apple cider vinegar, and season with salt.

Add the avocado, cucumber, and orange, and gently mix all ingredients together.

TIP For a perfect spa-lunch salad, add half of this finger salad with dressing to 2 cups leafy greens, ½ cup cooked chopped chicken, 1 tablespoon sesame seeds, and 1 tablespoon crumbled feta. Toss and serve, while you close your eyes and pretend you are at your own spa. Om.

These mini quiches not only give your baby a healthy serving of iron, protein, calcium, and fiber, they are also fun to eat. Most toddlers find food in a mini version to be virtually irresistible and will go crazy for them. Stuffing each serving of this mini quiche with a big helping of green vegetables will likely have you going bonkers for this recipe as well. If your child isn't a fan of the vegetables used in this recipe, substitute any vegetables you have on hand or ones you know your toddler will happily devour.

Green Veggie-Loaded Mini Quiche

12+ MONTHS

MAKES 24 mini quiches
PREP TIME: 15 minutes
COOK TIME: 25 minutes

STORAGE
Refrigerator: 3 days
Freezer: 2 months

Cooking spray

2 tablespoons finely chopped leeks

3 stems asparagus, finely chopped

½ cup finely chopped spinach, stems removed

2 green onions, finely chopped

4 eggs plus 1 yolk

½ cup plain Greek yogurt

¼ cup whole milk

1 tablespoon whole-wheat bread crumbs

Freshly ground black pepper

1 cup shredded Gruyère or sharp white Cheddar cheese

Preheat the oven to 400°F. Spray a mini muffin pan with cooking spray.

In a small bowl, add the leeks, asparagus, spinach, and green onions.

In a medium bowl, whip eggs, yogurt, milk, and bread crumbs until just incorporated. Season with pepper.

Put a small layer of cheese at the bottom of the each cup in the muffin pan for the crust.

Add roughly 1 teaspoon of vegetable mix on top of the cheese in each cup.

Pour the egg mixture into the cups until they are ⅔ full.

Add another layer of cheese on top of the egg mixture.

Sprinkle each cup with pepper.

Place the muffin tin in the oven, and bake for 20 minutes, or until the cheese is melted and bubbly.

Let the muffins cool for 5 minutes in the muffin pan, and then transfer them, individually, to a wire rack.

TIP For grown-ups: serve quiche with a large mixed green salad tossed with green onions, sliced raw zucchini, and pumpkin seeds in a balsamic vinaigrette.

Before my first child, I had eaten meatballs a total of zero times. Yes, zero! As difficult as that is to believe, my baby and I began eating meatballs together. Since then I've become a meatball enthusiast and eat them almost on a weekly basis. I like to make them in different sizes: small for first finger foods, medium for toddlers attempting to use a fork, large for grown-ups, or a mixture of them all. This recipe is my favorite hands-off way to cook Italian-style meatballs. With minimal prep time you can make these in the morning before work—or during your baby's nap time—and have a warm meal ready, stress-free, that night.

Easy Slow Cooker Mini Meatballs + Marinara Sauce

12+ MONTHS

MAKES 4 (4 meatball) servings
PREP TIME: 10 minutes
COOK TIME: up to 6 hours

STORAGE
Refrigerator: 4 days
Freezer: 4 months

FOR THE MARINARA SAUCE

2 (28-ounce) cans crushed tomatoes

2 tablespoons olive oil

½ yellow onion, diced

2 garlic cloves, minced

1 tablespoon dried basil

1 teaspoon dried oregano

½ teaspoon crushed red peppers

1 teaspoon salt

FOR THE MEATBALLS

1 pound lean ground chicken or mixture of ground beef and pork

½ cup whole-wheat bread crumbs

2 garlic cloves, minced

1 tablespoon dried basil

1 tablespoon dried parsley

½ cup Parmesan cheese

1 egg, beaten

In a slow cooker, mix together the crushed tomatoes, olive oil, onion, garlic, basil, oregano, crushed peppers, and salt.

In a medium bowl, combine the meat, bread crumbs, garlic, basil, parsley, cheese, and egg. Shape into 16 mini balls, using clean wet hands if the meat starts to stick.

Place the meatballs in the slow cooker on top of the marinara sauce, gently dunking the meatballs into the sauce.

Cover and set the slow cooker on low for 4 to 6 hours.

Serve over a favorite pasta, on a whole-wheat bun, or as a finger food.

....

WINE PAIRING TIP I might be a little biased because of my year in Florence, but spaghetti-and-meatball night is Chianti night at my house! The husband and I will buy any vintage after 2002.

....

Everything sounds better in French, doesn't it? *Pain de viande* simply means meatloaf. For years, I was dubious that my refined palate (not to mention the unpredictable one of my first child) could enjoy boring, dry, and—let's face it—ugly meatloaf. But just as you can dress it up with a new French identity, you can also spice it up with some special ingredients. It took a few attempts, but this modern meatloaf with kale, apricot, and sage really sings. It's not too hard on the eyes, either.

Pain de Viande Moderne

12+ MONTHS

MAKES 8 large servings
PREP TIME: 15 minutes
COOK TIME: 45 minutes

STORAGE
Refrigerator: 4 days
Freezer: 2 months

Cooking spray

1 large egg

1 tablespoon Greek yogurt

1 cup old-fashioned oats

½ cup whole-wheat bread crumbs

¼ cup tomato paste

1 tablespoon honey

4 apricots, thawed if frozen, cut in half and pitted

3 kale leaves, roughly torn

1 carrot, peeled and grated

1 pound ground chicken, lean

Sea salt

Freshly ground black pepper

Preheat the oven to 350°F. Spray a large loaf pan with cooking spray.

In a large bowl, whisk the egg, Greek yogurt, oats, and bread crumbs together. Set aside.

In a food processor, blend the tomato paste, honey, and apricots together. Set aside ½ cup of the sauce.

Add the kale to the remaining sauce in the food processor, and pulse until the kale is well incorporated.

Add the kale sauce, carrot, and chicken into the large bowl, and mix well.

Season the chicken mixture well with salt and pepper.

CONTINUED

PAIN DE VIANDE MODERNE

···

continued

Scoop the chicken mixture out of the bowl and into the loaf pan. Pat the mixture down until it is even on top.

Pour the reserved sauce onto the chicken loaf.

Bake for 45 minutes or until an inserted knife comes out clean.

Let the loaf cool and serve.

TIP I like to serve this with a tall glass of milk. When shopping for your family, look for organic milk from grass-fed cows, as this is higher in nutritional content than milk from conventionally raised, grain-fed cows. Benefits include higher levels of fat-soluble vitamins A, D, E, and K and of essential fatty acids crucial to the proper nervous system and brain development of children, including conjugated linoleic acid (CLA), which has many health benefits and is found only in grass-fed meat.

Made in one dish with no browning time, this simple and classic stew is perfect comfort food for your toddler, not to mention a snap for Mom! Chunky pieces of beef, carrots, potatoes, and mushrooms simmered in a light broth with a subtle hint of thyme will give your toddler a complete meal that can be eaten with a big kid's spoon, a fork, or just plain fingers.

Toddler Beef Stew

12+ MONTHS

MAKES 6 servings
PREP TIME: 15 minutes
COOK TIME: 3 hours

STORAGE
Refrigerator: 3 days
Freezer: 2 months

2 pounds beef chuck, trimmed and cut into 1½-inch pieces

1 teaspoon salt

1 teaspoon freshly ground black pepper

2 tablespoons all-purpose flour

2 bay leaves

4 sprigs fresh thyme, roughly chopped

2 cloves garlic, minced

1 medium onion, finely chopped

3 medium carrots, peeled and chopped into discs

4 medium white potatoes, chopped into quarters

12 whole cremini mushrooms, stems removed and cut in half

1 cup red wine (or double the stock amount)

1 cup beef stock

2 teaspoons balsamic vinegar

1 tablespoon finely chopped fresh parsley

Preheat the oven to 275°F.

In a medium bowl, add the beef, salt, pepper, and flour. Stir until beef is generously coated, and then dust off any excess flour.

In a casserole dish or Dutch oven, place the beef, bay leaves, thyme, garlic, onion, carrots, potatoes, mushrooms, wine, beef stock, and balsamic vinegar; then stir and cover with a tight-fitting lid.

Place the dish in the oven and cook for 2½ to 3 hours, stirring occasionally, adding additional stock if needed. Remove bay leaves, and let cool slightly.

Garnish with parsley, and serve with a crusty loaf of bread along with—for grown-ups—a simple green salad.

TIP Rest assured, when wine is cooked at a high temperature for a long period of time, all the alcohol evaporates, while leaving only its delicious flavor behind, making the dish safe for a child to eat.

Come fall, you can usually find me Sunday nights in the kitchen roasting vegetables (with a glass of wine in hand) for an easy, warm, and filling dinner. While I tend to roast whatever I have left over from the week, this combination is one of my family's favorites, mixing crunchy Brussels sprouts, caramelized chunks of sweet potatoes, and tart dried cranberries, all served over chewy quinoa.

Roasted Fall Veggies + Dried Cranberries

12+ MONTHS

MAKES 4 servings
PREP TIME: 10 minutes
COOK TIME: 40 minutes

STORAGE
Refrigerator: 4 days

FOR THE ROASTED VEGETABLES

2 tablespoons olive oil

1 tablespoon maple syrup

2 teaspoons paprika

1 teaspoon chili powder

½ teaspoon sea salt

½ teaspoon ground nutmeg

3 cups Brussels sprouts, ends removed
    and quartered

2 small sweet potatoes, peeled and cubed

¼ cup dried cranberries

FOR THE QUINOA

2 cups water

1 cup uncooked quinoa, well washed

FOR THE DRESSING

1 tablespoon grain mustard

1 tablespoon maple syrup

1 tablespoon olive oil

1 teaspoon orange zest

Salt

Freshly ground black pepper

Preheat the oven to 350°F. Line a baking sheet with foil or parchment paper.

In a medium bowl, whisk together the olive oil, maple syrup, paprika, chili powder, sea salt, and nutmeg. Add the Brussels sprouts and the sweet potatoes, and mix until well combined. Pour onto the baking sheet, and cook for 30 to 40 minutes or until golden brown, stirring halfway through baking time.

Meanwhile, in a medium saucepan, bring water and quinoa to a boil over high heat. Reduce heat to low, cover, and simmer for 15 to 20 minutes, or until all the water is absorbed.

In a small bowl, whisk the mustard, maple syrup, olive oil, orange zest, and season with salt and pepper.

Combine Brussels sprouts, sweet potatoes, and dried cranberries, and serve over the quinoa. Drizzle with dressing, and serve.

....

TIP Roasted veggies served with pecan-encrusted, pan-fried chicken makes a superb family meal. The warm spices and dried cranberries pair nicely with a light bodied, silky, and spicy glass of Pinot Noir. Some of my favorite Pinot Noirs come from the Anderson Valley region in California.

....

Don't let the long prep time scare you off this recipe, as there's actually very little hands-on time involved. These baked tofu sticks are crispy on the outside, smooth on the inside, and super delicious dunked into a creamy peanut dipping sauce. Since you are going to have some hands-free time in the kitchen you can whip up some Vegetable "Fried" Rice (page 141) for a nice side dish, and the Bumpin' Banana "Milkshake" (page 112) for dessert. See how nicely that all worked out!

Sesame Tofu Sticks + Peanut Sauce

12+ MONTHS

MAKES 4 small servings with
1 cup dipping sauce
PREP TIME: 45 minutes
COOK TIME: 40 minutes

STORAGE
Refrigerator: 3 days
Freezer: Not recommended

FOR THE TOFU STICKS

Cooking spray

14-ounce tofu, sprouted firm or extra firm

1 tablespoon sesame oil

3 tablespoons soy sauce

2 teaspoons rice vinegar

2 tablespoons honey

1-inch piece fresh ginger, grated

1 garlic clove, minced

2 tablespoons sesame seeds

FOR THE PEANUT SAUCE

½ cup creamy peanut butter

½ cup warm water

1 tablespoon soy sauce

1 lime, juiced

2 tablespoons brown sugar or honey

Pinch cayenne (optional)

Preheat the oven to 400°F. Grease a baking dish or sheet with cooking spray.

Cut the tofu lengthwise into 2 long pieces, and place on top of a stack of paper towels. Place another layer of paper towels on top of the tofu, and stack something heavy (books, cast iron skillet, baking sheet, kettle) on top to release any extra moisture. Let sit for 10 minutes. Replace the paper towels, and repeat the process for an additional 10 minutes.

CONTINUED

SESAME TOFU STICKS + PEANUT SAUCE

....

continued

While the tofu is pressing, in a medium bowl whisk together the sesame oil, soy sauce, vinegar, honey, ginger, and garlic.

When the tofu is done pressing, cut into stick or nugget shapes. Place the tofu in the medium bowl with the marinade. Let stand for 20 minutes, rotating halfway through.

Place the tofu on the baking sheet in a single layer, and sprinkle with sesame seeds.

Bake for 40 minutes, flipping the sticks halfway through.

Meanwhile, in a medium bowl, whisk together the peanut butter and water until smooth. Add in the soy sauce, lime juice, brown sugar, and cayenne pepper, and mix until well combined.

This vegetable "fried" rice is a regular in our house because it tastes just like our favorite take-out version but is easier on the calories and salt and is loaded with extra veggies. When making rice, I always double the amount I need so I can freeze a batch for those moments I'm short on time. This recipe uses this pre-cooked rice and is perfect meal for a busy weekday. If you don't have any frozen precooked rice on hand, instant or quick-cooking rice works equally well.

Vegetable "Fried" Rice

12+ MONTHS

MAKES 4 large servings
PREP TIME: 10 minutes
COOK TIME: 15 minutes

STORAGE
Refrigerator: 3 days
Freezer: Not recommended

2 tablespoons sesame oil, divided

2 garlic cloves, minced

1-inch piece fresh ginger, grated

2 eggs, whisked

3 cups cooked brown rice

½ cup corn, frozen

½ cup peas, frozen

½ cup shelled, frozen edamame

½ cup peeled and shredded carrot

2 tablespoons soy sauce

In a large pan, heat 1 tablespoon of sesame oil over medium heat. Add garlic and ginger, and cook for 1 to 2 minutes. Pour in the eggs, and cook by gently pushing them around the pan for 1 to 2 minutes.

Add the rice and remaining tablespoon of oil, stirring until everything is incorporated and sticking together.

Add corn, peas, edamame, carrot, and soy sauce, and fry for another 3 to 5 minutes, until all vegetables are cooked.

Let cool slightly and serve.

TIP Sometimes toddlers like the simple things in life—this simple Asian cucumber salad is one of them. It's easy to prepare while the main meal is coming together. In a small bowl, mix together 1 thinly sliced Persian cucumber, ¼ finely chopped red pepper, 1 teaspoon sesame oil, 1 teaspoon rice vinegar, and a sprinkle of sesame seeds.

Those days of jetting off to Morocco on a moment's notice (if only . . .) are long gone. With that in mind, I humbly offer a slow cooker Moroccan tagine that will transport you to North Africa in the comfort of your own home. The slow cooker gradually brings together all of the intense, rich spices into a magically sweet and complex sauce. Before I even had a moment to debate whether this was perhaps too much for my toddler, she had devoured her entire bowl and was asking for more.

Slow Cooker Chicken Tagine + Couscous

12+ MONTHS

MAKES 8 servings
PREP TIME: 25 minutes
COOK TIME: up to 8 hours

STORAGE
Refrigerator: 3 days
Freezer: Not recommended

FOR THE CHICKEN

1 tablespoon olive oil

2 pounds chicken breasts or thighs, or mixture or both, cut in 1-inch-cubed pieces

2 cups low-sodium chicken stock

2 tablespoons tomato paste

2 tablespoons lemon juice

2 teaspoons ground cumin

2 teaspoons ground coriander

1½ teaspoons ground ginger

1 teaspoon ground cinnamon

½ teaspoon ground turmeric

¼ teaspoon ground cloves

¼ teaspoon cayenne pepper

Salt

Freshly ground black pepper

½ yellow onion, finely chopped

3 large carrots, peeled and finely chopped

¼ cup dried cranberries

¼ cup chopped, dried apricots

FOR THE COUSCOUS

1 cup water

1 cup couscous

In a medium skillet, heat the olive oil over medium heat, and cook the chicken pieces for 5 minutes, or until all sides are browned but the pieces are not cooked through.

In the slow cooker, stir together the chicken stock, tomato paste, lemon juice, cumin, coriander, ginger, cinnamon, turmeric, cloves, and cayenne pepper, and season with salt and pepper.

Add in the chicken, onion, carrots, cranberries, and apricots to the slow cooker, and heat on low for 6 to 8 hours or high for 3 to 4 hours.

To make the couscous, in a small saucepan bring the water to a boil, stir in the couscous, and remove from heat. Cover, and let stand for 5 minutes. Fluff with a fork before serving.

Divide the couscous into bowls, and spoon a big heaping of chicken tagine on top.

COCKTAIL PAIRING TIP Let Morocco inspire a refreshing cocktail for the parents. Shake together 2 ounces of pomegranate vodka, ½ ounce simple syrup (see the recipe below), ½ ounce lemon juice, and ½ ounce pomegranate juice in a cocktail shaker filled with ice. Strain into a chilled glass.

To make simple syrup, in a small saucepan, bring 1 cup water, ¼ cup cardamom seeds, 2 cups sugar, and 5 mint leaves to a boil, and stir until sugar is dissolved. Strain and let cool before using.

The old-school shepherd's pie gets a reboot in a healthy yet irresistible stick-to-your-ribs-on-a-cold-day kind of way. It all starts with a base of nutritious ground turkey, parsnips, carrots, and peas, simmered with a zesty pinch of chili and allspice, then topped with tantalizing mashed sweet potatoes— I know I had you at mashed sweet potatoes. There is a reason some recipes stick around forever. Let's think of this one as a new-school version of an old-school classic.

Healthy Shepherd's Pie + Mashed Sweet Potatoes

12+ MONTHS

MAKES 6 servings
PREP TIME: 15 minutes
COOK TIME: 70 minutes

STORAGE
Refrigerator: 4 days
Freezer: 2 months

Cooking spray

2 large sweet potatoes, peeled, cubed

2 garlic cloves, 1 whole, 1 minced, divided

2 tablespoons olive oil, divided

1 pound ground turkey or chicken

½ onion, diced

2 carrots, peeled and chopped

1 parsnip, peeled and chopped

1 cup peas, frozen and thawed

1 cup chicken broth or water

2 teaspoons tomato paste

1 teaspoon roughly chopped thyme

¼ teaspoon ground allspice

½ teaspoon chili powder

Salt

Freshly ground black pepper

½ cup milk

Paprika, for garnish

Preheat the oven to 400°F. Grease 1 pie pan or 6 individual ramekins with cooking spray.

In a medium saucepan, cover the sweet potato chunks and 1 garlic clove with water, and bring to a boil over high heat. Turn heat to medium-low, and cook for 15 to 20 minutes, or until potatoes are tender. Drain, let cool, and set aside.

In a large skillet, heat 1 tablespoon olive oil over medium heat, add the turkey, and cook for 10 minutes or until brown, breaking the turkey down into small pieces with the back of a spoon. Place the cooked turkey on a plate, and set aside.

CONTINUED

HEALTHY SHEPHERD'S PIE + MASHED SWEET POTATOES

continued

Add the remaining tablespoon olive oil into the skillet and heat over medium heat. Add the onion and cook for 3 to 5 minutes or until translucent. Add the minced garlic and cook for 1 more minute. Add in the carrots and the parsnip, and cook for another 10 minutes.

Add the cooked turkey, peas, chicken broth, tomato paste, thyme, allspice, and chili powder, and cook on low for 5 minutes. Season with salt and pepper.

In a medium bowl, using a blender, take the cooked sweet potatoes and the garlic, and mix well with milk.

In the pie dish or individual ramekins, first spoon a layer of the meat mixture, followed by a layer of mashed sweet potatoes. Sprinkle the top of the potatoes with paprika.

Bake for 20 minutes. Let cool and serve.

TIP I love using individual ramekins or mugs for family dinners. My toddler loves that she gets her own ("Mine! Mine! Mine!") cute dish, and I love that I can easily freeze the leftovers for another meal.

This quick and comforting dish was the first meal Ellie really dove into full force: face hovering above her plate, elbows deep into the sauce, barely taking a break from shoveling the pasta into her little mouth. Though I would like to say she has cleaned up her eating habits, as of now, she hasn't. This simple meal of good ground beef simmered with mushrooms in a thyme-spiced Stroganoff sauce is one of her favorite meals. Now where did I put that full-body bib...?

Beef Stroganoff

12+ MONTHS

MAKES 4 servings
PREP TIME: 10 minutes
COOK TIME: 25 minutes

STORAGE
Refrigerator: 3 days
Freezer: Not recommended

1 tablespoon olive oil

1 pound ground beef, sirloin preferred

½ medium onion, chopped

8 ounces sliced fresh mushrooms, stems removed

2 garlic cloves, minced

1 teaspoon salt

1½ teaspoon freshly ground black pepper

2 tablespoons all-purpose flour

1 cup low-sodium chicken broth

1 teaspoon finely chopped fresh thyme

½ cup sour cream

8 ounces extra-wide egg noodles

1 tablespoon butter

2 tablespoons finely chopped fresh parsley

In a large skillet, heat the olive oil over medium-high heat. Brown the ground sirloin, stirring occasionally to break up the meat, for 8 minutes or until golden brown. Remove and set aside.

Turn the heat down to medium, add the onion and mushrooms to the skillet, and cook for 3 to 5 minutes or until the onions are tender, stirring frequently. Add in the garlic, and cook for 2 more minutes. Stir in the salt, pepper, and flour, and cook for another minute.

Put the ground sirloin back into the skillet, and add the broth and thyme, stirring often, for 8 to 10 minutes or until the sauce has thickened. Turn the heat down to low, and stir in the sour cream.

Bring a large pot of salted water to a boil over high heat, and cook the egg noodles as directed by the package. Drain, toss lightly with the butter, and put into a large serving bowl.

Spoon the meat sauce over the noodles, and garnish with the parsley.

The first and last time I ate frozen fish sticks, I was nine. They were so bad it scared me off from eating fish for years. Flash forward 20-plus years (gulp) and I decided to give fish sticks another shot. This time it was on my terms: flaky white fish encrusted in a crunchy coconut and panko crust, gently pan-fried to perfection. There were amazing—so amazing, that when Ellie stole a piece off my plate, I almost stole it back!

Coconut Fish Sticks +
Thai Curry Dipping Sauce

12+ MONTHS

MAKES 4 servings
PREP TIME: 10 minutes
COOK TIME: 15 minutes

STORAGE
Refrigerator: 3 days
Freezer: Not recommended

FOR THE FISH STICKS

1½ cups shredded toasted coconut

1 cup panko bread crumbs

½ cup whole-wheat flour

2 eggs

2 teaspoons soy sauce

1 pound fish (tilapia, halibut, or cod), cut into 2-inch-long strips

Salt

Freshly ground black pepper

2 tablespoons olive oil or coconut oil, divided

FOR THE THAI CURRY DIPPING SAUCE

1 teaspoon curry powder

⅛ teaspoon red pepper flakes

1 tablespoon honey

½ orange, juiced

¼ cup sour cream or mayonnaise

In a small shallow bowl, whisk together the coconut, panko, and flour. In another small shallow bowl, whisk together the eggs and soy sauce.

Dip each piece of fish first into the egg mixture, and then into the coconut mixture, patting each piece until completely covered. Place fish sticks on a plate. Repeat until all pieces are coated. Sprinkle with salt and pepper.

In a medium skillet, heat 1 tablespoon of oil over medium heat. Let the oil get hot. Cook half of the fish sticks for 3 minutes on each side, or until golden brown and cooked all the way through. Place the fish sticks on a paper towel to soak up any excess oil.

Heat the remaining 1 tablespoon of oil, and repeat with the remaining fish sticks.

To make the sauce, in a small bowl, whisk together the curry, red pepper flakes, honey, orange juice, and sour cream until well incorporated.

TIP I like to serve these fish sticks with a healthy side that is also easy to dunk into this yummy Thai dipping sauce: steamed broccoli, green beans, or carrot sticks. For a special treat, I like to make homemade baked "chips" that complement the fish sticks as well.

One night I was desperate to get something—anything—on the table. I wasn't trying to be particularly healthy or fancy. It shouldn't be possible to achieve such amazingly creamy pasta without cheese, butter, or cream, but it is, thanks entirely to butternut squash. Your picky toddler (and everyone else at the table) might go vegan after this one.

Vegan Butternut Squash "Mac + Cheese"

12+ MONTHS

MAKES 6 large servings
PREP TIME: 5 minutes
COOK TIME: 55 minutes

STORAGE
Refrigerator: 3 days

1 medium butternut squash, cut in half

1 (12-ounce) box of pasta

1 tablespoon olive oil

½ yellow onion, diced

2 garlic cloves, minced

½ teaspoon curry powder

1 teaspoon fresh thyme

1 cup vegetable broth

Sea salt

Freshly ground black pepper

TIP The most time-consuming part of this dish is roasting the squash. If you are usually in a time crunch at dinner (and who isn't?), you can purchase cubed butternut squash, in fresh or frozen form, and it'll cook in minutes.

Preheat the oven to 400°F. Line a baking sheet with parchment paper or a silicon mat.

Place the butternut squash on the baking sheet, skin-side down. Bake for 40 minutes or until a fork can easily prick the skin.

Meanwhile, bring a large pot of water to a boil. Add the pasta, and cook according to the package directions.

In a large skillet, heat the olive oil over medium heat. Add the onion and cook for 3 to 5 minutes or until translucent. Add the garlic, and cook for an additional 2 minutes.

Take the butternut squash out of the oven, and let it cool enough until you can handle it.

Scrape the squash from the skin, and place it in a blender or food processor. Add the cooked onion and garlic, curry powder, thyme, and broth, and purée until smooth.

Return the squash to the skillet, and heat over medium heat until warm. Add the pasta, and season with salt and pepper. Stir until all ingredients are well combined. Serve immediately.

These bright green falafel patties are a great vegetarian option for giving your baby protein—plus some extra iron from the spinach! Bursting with flavor, these patties are loaded with nutrient-full parsley, spinach, chickpeas, and garlic. Pan-frying them in a little olive oil provides some extra healthy fat and flavor, while making them crispy on the outside and delicately tender on the inside. A perfect handheld meal for babes any time of day.

Spinach + Parsley Falafel Patties

12+ MONTHS

MAKES 4 small servings
PREP TIME: 5 minutes
COOK TIME: 15 minutes

STORAGE
Refrigerator: 3 days
Freezer: Not recommended

2 cups trimmed and roughly chopped, packed spinach

¼ cup roughly chopped fresh parsley

1 (15½-ounce) can chickpeas, drained and rinsed

2 gloves garlic, minced

1 tablespoon tahini

½ lemon, juiced

½ teaspoon ground cumin

¼ teaspoon paprika

Salt

Freshly ground black pepper

3 tablespoons whole-wheat flour

4 tablespoons olive oil

Place the spinach, parsley, chickpeas, garlic, tahini, lemon juice, cumin, and paprika in a food processor and season with salt and pepper. Pulse in 2-second increments until well combined.

Transfer the mix to a mixing bowl, and stir in the flour, 1 tablespoon at a time until the falafel mixture is thick enough to handle.

In a large skillet, heat half of the olive oil over medium-high heat. Add half of the patties, or as many as will fit comfortably in the pan, and cook for 3 to 4 minutes, checking once to make sure they are not browning too fast. Flip the patties and cook for another 3 to 4 minutes, or until golden brown on both sides.

Heat the additional olive oil and continue until all patties are cooked.

Serve immediately.

Okay, call me out—I'm ready for it. Officially, I recommend not sneaking veggies into food. But sometimes it just makes sense (and boy does it work). I guess I'm of the school of thought that says to learn the rules first, then break them on occasion. This tomato sauce breaks the rules in all the best ways. It tastes just like a regular tomato sauce but is filled with red peppers, leeks, and carrots. You can serve it chunky or puréed smooth depending on how you use it. You earn a gold star if you top the sauce with even more vegetables and a double gold star if your toddler devours it.

Easy Veggie-Filled Tomato Sauce

12+ MONTHS

MAKES 6 cups
PREP TIME: 15 minutes
COOK TIME: 50 minutes

STORAGE
Refrigerator: 3 days
Freezer: 2 months

1 tablespoon olive oil

½ small onion, diced

1 small leek, green and white parts, roughly chopped

1 carrot, peeled and chopped

½ red bell pepper, seeded and chopped

1 stick celery, roughly chopped

1 (28-ounce) can diced tomatoes

1 cup water, vegetable or chicken stock

1 teaspoon dried basil

1 teaspoon dried parsley

¼ teaspoon red chili pepper flakes

¼ cup feta (optional)

Salt

Freshly ground black pepper

In a large saucepan, heat the olive oil over medium-low heat. Add the onion and let cook for 5 minutes or until translucent.

Add the leek, carrot, red pepper, and celery, and cook for 10 minutes, until the vegetables are tender.

Add in the tomatoes, stock, basil, parsley, and pepper flakes, and turn heat to high, bring to a boil, and then simmer on low for 30 minutes, stirring occasionally. Let cool slightly.

Using a hand mixture or blender, purée until slightly chunky or smooth. Pour the sauce back into the saucepan and heat on low.

Stir in the feta until melted. Season with salt and pepper.

While everyone has their own personal chili they hold near and dear to their hearts, this is my favorite for toddlers. It's heavy on the chunks and light on the broth, making it a little easier for toddlers to eat: beans, ground turkey, corn, carrots, and whole-wheat pasta all simmered together in a traditional red chili sauce. Serve with mini corn-bread muffins and your favorite toppings for a family meal that's always a winner.

Tot Chili

12+ MONTHS

MAKES 8 servings
PREP TIME: 15 minutes
COOK TIME: 90 minutes

STORAGE
Refrigerator: 3 days
Freezer: Not recommended

1 tablespoon olive oil

½ yellow onion, chopped

2 garlic cloves, minced

1 pound ground meat (or 12 ounces soy crumbles or shredded tempeh)

2 carrots, peeled and thinly sliced

2 tablespoons chili powder

¼ teaspoon nutmeg

¼ teaspoon paprika

¼ teaspoon cloves

1 (15-ounce) can pinto beans, drained and rinsed

1 (15-ounce) can dark kidney beans, drained and rinsed

1 (15-ounce) can corn, drained and rinsed

1 (15-ounce) can diced tomatoes

1 (15-ounce) can chicken or vegetable stock

1½ cup whole-wheat elbow pasta

2 tablespoons roughly chopped cilantro

Salt

Freshly ground black pepper

In a large saucepan, heat the olive oil over medium heat. Add the onion, and cook for 5 minutes or until translucent. Add the garlic, and cook for another 2 to 3 minutes. Add ground meat, and cook for 10 minutes or until brown, breaking down big clumps with the back of wooden spoon.

Add the carrots, chili powder, nutmeg, paprika, and cloves, and cook for 3 to 5 minutes, stirring to make sure everything is well incorporated.

Add the beans, corn, tomatoes, and stock. Bring to a boil over high heat, then reduce to simmer, and cook for 45 to 60 minutes.

Pour in the pasta and cilantro, season with salt and pepper, and cook for another 15 minutes or until pasta is done.

Let cool slightly, and serve with your favorite toppings.

I know you get it when I say we all have "those nights"—you know, when you forgot to take the chicken out of the freezer, or you thought you'd have time to swing by the market on your way home, or you got caught in a traffic jam three blocks from your house. It happens to us all. That's why I always keep a box of mac and cheese in my pantry, just for these sort of emergencies. I don't stress about it, I just get to work finding ingredients in my fridge and pantry I can add to the pasta for a little healthy kick. This bright green add-in with spinach, broccoli, and basil is my family's favorite. If you don't have fresh basil on hand, a tablespoon of pesto is another great option.

Super Power Mac + Cheese

12+ MONTHS

MAKES 3 small servings
PREP TIME: 5 minutes
COOK TIME: 15 minutes

STORAGE
Refrigerator: 3 days
Freezer: Not recommended

1 box white Cheddar cheese shells

½ cup packed spinach

½ cup packed basil

¼ cup broccoli florets

1 garlic clove

1 tablespoon olive oil

1 tablespoon butter

¼ cup milk

Bring a large pot of salted water to a boil over high heat. Cook the shells according to package directions.

In a food processor or blender, place the spinach, basil, broccoli, garlic, and the olive oil, and purée for 1 to 3 minutes, or until just slightly chunky. Scrape down sides of the food processor as needed.

In a large pot, over low heat, whisk the butter, milk, and cheese packet until combined and creamy. Add the spinach and broccoli mixture and pasta, and stir until all the ingredients are incorporated.

Serve with a side of fruit for the kids and a simple mixed green salad and a big glass of wine for the grown-ups.

This do-it-yourself fiesta bowl feast is my go-to recipe when things are about to get real crazy at my house—as in hungry toddler, crying baby, nothing-planned-for-dinner crazy. I put my toddler in charge of attempting to spoon ingredients into bowls, my husband on tortilla chip/music duty, and I get busy slicing and dicing all the produce. Everyone gets to have a say in what their bowl looks like, which makes everyone happy in no time at all.

DIY Fiesta Bowl

12+ MONTHS

MAKES 4 servings
PREP TIME: 15 minutes
COOK TIME: 15 minutes

STORAGE
Refrigerator: 3 days
Freezer: Not recommended

FOR THE BASE OF THE BOWLS

2 cups cooked or instant brown rice

Juice of 1 lime

1 tablespoon olive oil

2 tablespoons roughly chopped cilantro

FOR OPTIONAL ADD-INS

Black beans, drained and rinsed

Corn, fresh or frozen, thawed and warmed

Red bell pepper, chopped

Green bell peppers, onions, and/or zucchini, sliced or chopped, and sautéed

Avocado, pitted, sliced, and chopped

Tomato, diced

Romaine lettuce, shredded

Salsa

Cheddar or pepper jack cheese, shredded

Sour cream or plain yogurt

Cooked ground turkey

Shredded, cooked chicken

Warmed tortillas

Corn chips

Pumpkin seeds

In a medium saucepan over medium heat, add the brown rice, lime juice, olive oil, and cilantro. Cook for 5 minutes, and then fluff.

Add ¼ cup of the rice mixture to each bowl. Add optional ingredients based on what you have on hand or your family's personal preferences.

Serve immediately, or warm before serving if necessary.

TIP Got a picky eater? Invite help in the kitchen. Toddlers love to help out, from tasks as simple as throwing out packaging to mixing ingredients. They're also more likely to end up eating the fruits (or veggies) of their shared labor.

I am the queen of chicken strips. Cannot. Get. Enough. I wanted a recipe that would rival my favorite fried version: moist on the inside and crispy on the outside, all with a creamy ranch dipping sauce. This recipe hits the mark! The key is to marinate the chicken strips in the ranch dressing before coating them with extra-crunchy panko bread crumbs. In the end, I ate four strips, while Ellie ate a half—I'm calling that a win.

Baked Ranch Chicken Strips + Dipping Sauce

12+ MONTHS

MAKES 4 small servings
PREP TIME: 40 minutes
COOK TIME: 20 minutes

STORAGE
Refrigerator: 3 days
Freezer: 2 months

FOR THE RANCH SAUCE

½ cup mayonnaise

½ cup sour cream

½ cup buttermilk or full-fat milk

1 teaspoon finely chopped chives

1 teaspoon finely chopped parsley

1 teaspoon Worcestershire sauce

½ teaspoon dried dill weed

½ teaspoon garlic powder

¼ teaspoon onion powder

Salt

Freshly ground black pepper

FOR THE CHICKEN STRIPS

1½ pound skinless, boneless chicken breasts, cut into 2-inch strips

¾ cup of Ranch Sauce

Cooking spray

½ cup whole-wheat flour

1 teaspoon salt

¼ teaspoon cayenne pepper

Freshly ground black pepper

2 large eggs

2 cups panko bread crumbs

Preheat the oven to 400°F.

In a medium bowl, whisk together the mayonnaise, sour cream, buttermilk, chives, parsley, Worcestershire sauce, dill weed, garlic powder, onion powder, salt, and pepper.

Reserve ¾ cup of sauce, cover, and refrigerate until needed.

In the medium bowl, add the chicken strips to the sauce. Cover and place in the refrigerator for 30 minutes, and up to 8 hours.

Generously spray a baking sheet with cooking spray.

Combine the flour, salt, and cayenne pepper in a shallow bowl and season with black pepper. In another shallow bowl, beat the eggs. In a third shallow bowl, place the panko bread crumbs.

Take each chicken strip, and coat it first in the flour mixture, brushing off any excess, then the egg mixture, dripping off any excess, and then finally roll the strip in the panko. Place the chicken strips on the baking sheet, making sure they do not touch. Continue until all the strips are coated.

Spray each chicken strip with cooking spray, and bake for 20 minutes, flipping it halfway through the baking time.

Serve with cut carrots, celery, and extra ranch dipping sauce.

. . . .

TIP For a more "grown-up" meal, these chicken strips make a perfect Cobb salad. Layer 3 cups chopped romaine lettuce with ½ cup chopped avocado; 1 chopped, hard-boiled egg; 2 slices of crumbled bacon; 2 tablespoons blue cheese; ½ chopped tomato; ½ cup chopped cucumber; and 3 chopped chicken strips, all drizzled with 3 tablespoons ranch sauce. Now that's what I'm talking about!

. . . .

You guys, this baked dish is the one. My favorite of all favorites—well, at least my favorite of the healthy dishes, that's for sure. And while we are firm believers in quinoa, I think we've always stood in the great-as-a-side-dish-but-not-main-dish camp. But this recipe changes things. Here quinoa is mixed with cherry tomatoes, olives, spinach, and artichokes, and topped with not one but two types of cheese, then baked until it's all bubbly and happy and smells so good you want to stick your face right into it—which I don't recommend. I do, however, suggest you make this for your toddler, yourself, and everyone you know.

Cheesy Greek Quinoa Bake
WITH ARTICHOKES + OLIVES

12+ MONTHS

STORAGE
Refrigerator: 3 days
Freezer: 1 month

MAKES 6 small servings
PREP TIME: 10 minutes
COOK TIME: 40 minutes

2 cups water

1 cup dried quinoa

1 teaspoon salt

1 cup halved or quartered cherry tomatoes

1 cup trimmed and finely chopped packed spinach

1 cup roughly chopped marinated artichoke hearts

½ red onion, finely chopped

1 (2¼-ounce can) sliced black olives, drained

½ cup milk

1½ cups crumbled feta cheese, divided

2 garlic cloves, minced

1 teaspoon onion powder

1 teaspoon dried oregano

½ lemon, juiced

1 tablespoon olive oil

Salt

Freshly ground black pepper

1 cup shredded mozzarella cheese

1 tablespoon chopped fresh parsley

Preheat the oven to 400°F. Grease a small 8-by-8 casserole dish with cooking spray.

In a small saucepan, bring the water, quinoa, and salt to a boil. Cover, reduce heat to medium low, and simmer for 15 to 20 minutes, or until all the water is absorbed. Set aside, covered, for 5 minutes.

Meanwhile in a medium bowl, combine the tomatoes, spinach, artichoke hearts, red onion, olives, milk, 1 cup feta cheese, garlic, onion powder, oregano, lemon juice, and olive oil, until everything is well incorporated, and season with salt and pepper. Add in cooked quinoa and stir.

Pour the mixture into a casserole dish, and top with the remaining ½ cup feta, mozzarella, and parsley. Cook for 15 to 20 minutes, or until cheese is melted and the dish is heated through.

TIP This is a great dish to freeze for a quick dinner on a busy night, for a new mama meal, or for when your significant other is in charge of cooking. Once the ingredients are in the casserole dish, let it cool, then cover and freeze until needed. For best results, let it partially thaw overnight in the fridge, then bake in a preheated oven at 400°F, increasing the baking time until the dish is heated all the way through.

The first time I made this recipe, I ended up making it three times in a row—it was so good, we had to eat it every day. Served warm or cold, this mild cilantro pasta dish is bursting with both flavor and color (with three different types of veggies) and is a great way to change up your normal pasta routine.

Cilantro Pesto Pasta + Colorful Veggies

12+ MONTHS

MAKES 8 servings
PREP TIME: 10 minutes
COOK TIME: 15 minutes

STORAGE
Refrigerator: 3 days
Freezer: Not recommended

FOR THE CILANTRO PESTO

2 cups packed cilantro leaves

½ jalapeño pepper, seeded and roughly chopped

1 garlic clove, minced

½ cup raw almonds

¼ cup olive oil

1 tablespoon honey

1 lime, juiced

Salt

Freshly ground black pepper

FOR THE PASTA

1 package pasta of choice (bow-tie or ziti are great for toddlers)

1 cup fresh or frozen corn kernels

1 small zucchini, trimmed, sliced, and cut into quarters

1 cup halved or quartered grape tomatoes

2 tablespoons grated Parmesan cheese

In a food processor, combine the cilantro, jalapeño pepper, garlic, almonds, olive oil, honey, and lime juice until smooth, scraping down the sides when needed, and season with salt and pepper.

In a large pot, bring the water to a boil, and cook the pasta according to the package directions. Drain well and rinse under cold water. Transfer to a large serving bowl.

Add the corn, zucchini, tomatoes, and cilantro pesto to the pasta, and gently toss. Sprinkle with Parmesan. This dish is equally delicious served warm or cold as a summer salad.

TIP For some extra protein, try adding some cooked and crumbled jalapeño-flavored chicken or pork sausage.

I'm standing in the middle of the grocery store picking up some staples, when my baby gives me the "You have about 10 more seconds before I scream" look, while my toddler demands she needs a banana from our shopping cart. And I realize I have nothing planned for dinner. I quickly phone a friend, who gives me her latest recipe for polenta with sausage devoured by her toddler, Robby. Since Robby and Ellie are soul mates (in our minds, at least), I know it will be a hit at my house. I hang up looking forward to dinner—and my next night out with the girls.

Sausage + Kale over Creamy Polenta

12+ MONTHS

MAKES 3 servings
PREP TIME: 10 minutes
COOK TIME: 30 minutes

STORAGE
Refrigerator: 3 days
Freezer: Not recommended

FOR THE SAUSAGE AND KALE

1 tablespoon olive oil

3 Italian-flavored turkey or pork
    sausages, cut into ⅓-inch rounds

½ onion, finely chopped

2 garlic cloves, minced

½ teaspoon dried thyme

½ teaspoon ground cumin

½ bunch kale, stems removed, leaves torn
    into small bite-size pieces

1 cup canned crushed tomatoes

1 cup low-sodium chicken stock

¼ cup fresh parsley, for serving

Salt

Freshly ground black pepper

FOR THE POLENTA

3 cups water

½ teaspoon salt

1 cup polenta or cornmeal

1 tablespoon butter

In a large skillet, heat the olive oil over medium heat. Add the sausage and cook for 6 to 8 minutes, or until golden brown on both sides. Transfer the sausage to a plate and set aside.

Add the onion to the skillet, and cook for 3 to 5 minutes or until translucent. Add the garlic and cook for another minute. Add the thyme and cumin, and cook for an additional minute.

Add the kale and cook for 2 to 3 minutes, or until just beginning to wilt, stirring frequently. Add the tomatoes and chicken stock, and bring to a slight boil. Add in the sausage and parsley, season with salt and pepper, and simmer on low for 15 minutes.

Meanwhile, in a medium saucepan, bring the water and salt to a boil. Slowly add in the polenta, whisking the entire time. Reduce the heat so you get a few bubbles every couple of seconds, and cook for 20 to 30 minutes, vigorously stirring every 5 minutes or so to make sure the bottom isn't burning. When creamy, remove from the heat, and stir in the butter.

Spoon the polenta into individual bowls, then top with the sausage mixture. Sprinkle with parsley and serve.

....

TIP If the kale is still a little tough for your little one, feel free to substitute 2 cups of packed, trimmed spinach, or a half bunch of Swiss chard for the same results.

....

Pizza is a great dish for getting kids to eat vegetables they normally wouldn't. While this pizza starts with a base of spinach pesto, feel free to add any other vegetables of your toddler's choosing. My daughter will give almost any vegetable a try, if she can sprinkle on a little Parmesan.

Spinach Pesto Chicken Pita Pizza

12+ MONTHS

MAKES 6 pita pizzas
PREP TIME: 15 minutes
COOK TIME: 20 minutes

STORAGE
Refrigerator: 3 days
Freezer: Not recommended

FOR THE SPINACH PESTO

1 cup loosely packed spinach

½ cup fresh basil leaves

¼ cup raw almonds

¼ cup grated Parmesan cheese

1 garlic clove, minced

¼ teaspoon red pepper flakes

½ teaspoon salt

¼ teaspoon freshly ground black pepper

1 lemon, juiced

½ teaspoon lemon zest

¼ cup olive oil

FOR THE PIZZA

6 whole-wheat pita pockets

1 tablespoon olive oil

1 cup chicken, cooked, and cubed

2 tomatoes, sliced

2 cups grated mozzarella or Italian cheese blend

2 tablespoons pine nuts

Preheat the oven to 450°F.

In a food processor, combine all the pesto ingredients and pulse for 2 to 3 minutes. Scrape down the sides of the food processor as needed.

Place pita pockets onto a pizza stone or pan, and precook for 5 to 8 minutes or until just golden brown.

Brush the top of the pita pockets with olive oil, then top with the pesto, chicken, and tomatoes. Sprinkle cheese evenly over the entire pizza, and bake for 10 to 12 minutes, or until the cheese is brown and bubbly. Let cool for 2 to 3 minutes.

Sprinkle with pine nuts and serve.

TIP Trade in your normal glass of vino for an Italian aperitif called the Negroni. Mix one part gin, one part vermouth rosso, and one part Campari; garnish with an orange peel; and serve on the rocks. For a stylish twist on the original, top it off with a splash of Prosecco.

Lean in, I have to tell you a secret: this actually is a healthy dinner. Loaded with mashed sweet potatoes, spinach, black beans, and a pinch of cumin, then covered in melted white Cheddar and held together by whole-wheat tortillas, this quesadilla has it all. Even if your toddler refuses to eat it as a quesadilla and insists on opening it up to pick out her favorite goodies (beans, cheese, guacamole) one by one, it is still a nutritious meal I am happy to make us both.

Sweet Potato Quesadilla + Cilantro

12+ MONTHS

MAKES 4 small servings
PREP TIME: 15 minutes
COOK TIME: 15 minutes

STORAGE
Refrigerator: 3 days
Freezer: Not recommended

2 medium sweet potatoes

4 (8-inch) whole-wheat tortillas, or tortillas of choice

1 cup black beans, drained and rinsed

1 cup trimmed and finely chopped packed baby spinach

¼ purple onion, diced

2 tablespoons finely chopped cilantro

1 cup grated sharp white Cheddar cheese

1 teaspoon ground cumin

Cooking spray

1 cup guacamole, for serving

1 cup salsa, for serving

BEER PAIRING TIP These quesadillas will go well with a crisp lager for the 21 and over crowd. My husband loves Upslope Brewing Company's Craft Lager.

Prick the sweet potatoes several times with a fork, place on a microwave-safe plate, and microwave, uncovered, for 10 minutes. Let cool slightly.

Scoop out the sweet potato flesh, discarding the skin, and place in a small bowl. With a fork, smash the sweet potato until finely mashed.

On half of each of the tortillas, spread the mashed sweet potatoes, then top with beans, spinach, onion, cilantro, and cheese, and sprinkle with cumin. Fold the other half of tortilla over the filling.

Heat a large skillet over medium heat, and spray with cooking spray. Cook each quesadilla for 2 to 3 minutes on each side, or until golden brown and the cheese is melted.

Let cool slightly, and serve with your favorite guacamole and salsa.

Oven-baked eggs in a mild tomato salsa, black beans, and a bubbly brown cheese topping, all contained within a crispy tortilla—now that's what I call a good-for-you breakfast. These simple egg cups are my go-to recipe for fun Saturday breakfasts with the family. They're even my most requested dish for Christmas morning brunch. Regardless of the occasion, they're a crowd-pleaser for all ages.

Huevos Rancheros Cups

12+ MONTHS

MAKES: 12 servings
PREP TIME: 15 minutes
COOK TIME: 20 minutes

STORAGE
Refrigerator: 3 days
Freezer: 1 month

Cooking spray

½ jalapeño pepper, seeded

1 (14½-ounce) can fire-roasted tomatoes

½ white onion, roughly chopped

½ lime, juiced

½ teaspoon ground cumin

Salt

Freshly ground black pepper

12 (6-inch) corn or flour tortillas

2 tablespoons melted butter

1 cup black beans, drained, rinsed, and dried with paper towels

12 eggs

1 cup shredded pepper jack or Monterey Jack cheese

1 tablespoon fresh cilantro

1 avocado, peeled, pitted, and roughly chopped (optional)

2 tablespoons sour cream (optional)

Preheat the oven to 400°F. Spray a muffin tin generously with cooking spray.

In a food processor or blender, add the jalapeño pepper, tomatoes, onion, lime juice, and cumin, and purée until smooth. Season with salt and pepper.

Wrap half of the tortillas in a paper towel, and heat in the microwave for 20 to 30 seconds, or until warm and easy to bend.

Fit the tortillas snugly into each of the muffin tins, folding over parts of the tortilla, if needed. Brush each tortilla with a little butter, and sprinkle with salt

To construct the cups, layer first a heaping spoon of black beans, then a spoonful of the tomato sauce, and finish by cracking an egg into each cup. Sprinkle with salt and pepper.

Bake until the eggs are barely set, roughly 7 to 9 minutes. Top with the cheese, and bake for another 7 to 9 minutes until the cheese is bubbly and golden brown. Let cool slightly.

Sprinkle with cilantro, avocado, and a small dollop of sour cream.

....

COCKTAIL PAIRING TIP My fellow parents, you know that brunch just isn't brunch without a Bloody Mary. In a tall pitcher, mix together 6 ounces of premium vodka, 3 cups tomato juice, 6 tablespoons fresh lemon juice, 1 teaspoon horseradish, 1 teaspoon Worcestershire sauce, ¼ teaspoon salt, ¼ teaspoon pepper, and ¼ teaspoon Tabasco. Pour into tall glasses filled with ice, and garnish with a stalk of celery and a lemon wedge.

....

Dinner on Demand

(24+ MONTHS)

Frequently Asked Questions

Why is my toddler so picky all of a sudden?

Thankfully, there are developmental reasons why toddlers suddenly become picky, fussy, finicky, and fidgety at mealtimes. The first year of life is a year of rapid growth (and a lot of eating!), but from ages one to three children's growth slows relative to that first year. As a result, children actually need *less* food. Plus, toddlers are always running around, exploring, and learning—they don't spend much time sitting still, and so it's difficult for them to stop and sit at the table. All of these changes combined can make parents interpret their child's refusals to eat as pickiness when, in fact, toddlers are just more interested in doing other things, especially when you say it's dinnertime and their bodies don't signal hunger.

Toddlers also act stubborn when things don't go the way they want or expect. Your little one might be inclined to eat, but she'll get mad at you for putting the yellow plate at her place instead of asking her to choose which one she wants. Giving toddlers options is incredibly empowering for them—and often empowering enough to turn a picky kiddo into a willing eater.

Do everything you can to buy the right food, prepare it nutritiously, and create a fun and collaborative environment for meals and snacks. The rest is up to your child.

My toddler always wants to play at mealtime and is easily distracted at the table. What are some good tips for implementing more structure?

Ah, yes, meals with a toddler. A trip to the dentist might be more pleasant. The good news (sort of) is that mealtime is ultimately more stressful on you than on your little one. Here are some simple strategies to help with your sanity—oh, and your toddler's schedule. Try applying them to just one meal of the day, likely dinner.

Prepare your child for mealtime with a routine, such as hand washing and picking out her plate.

- Talk to your child about what you are preparing, noting the ingredients in the dish you already know she likes.

- Tell your child what you expect at mealtime, such as eating, sitting still, using table manners, and trying at least one bite of a new food.

- Offer limited but flexible choices, such as water or milk, roasted carrot or zucchini sticks, black beans or pinto beans, and so on.

- Try to resist the temptation to prepare something else if your child doesn't like what's being served.

- Let her participate in the meal by serving herself or letting her choosing what goes on the plate, and even where.

I make every effort to offer my child healthy foods, but between birthday parties, Halloween, and the holidays, the lure of junk food is hard to avoid. What can I do?

We all want our children to choose the veggies instead of the cheese puffs, but you already know all too well that we can't control everything. While you want to avoid giving your child junk food, you shouldn't forbid occasional treats either. Banning certain foods makes them more attractive, and more likely your child will over-indulge when she gets an opportunity to eat them at a friend's house, a birthday party, or at school.

It's good to have an ongoing discussion with your child about healthy foods and how they help them to do all the things they love to do, like playing, running, jumping, spinning in circles—all of it. Sometimes children *will* choose junk first, but sometimes they may surprise you and pick a fruit, veggie, or yogurt all on their own. As long as children are allowed to make choices and understand that certain foods are only "sometimes" foods, they are not likely to develop an unhealthy relationship with food, which is a much more worthy goal than passing over a cupcake at a party.

You will transform the everyday turkey burger with these colorful and kid-friendly beet, carrot, and cilantro patties. The added Greek yogurt not only provides extra protein, but helps keep the smaller burgers moist and juicy. Serve them with or without a bun, and watch as your kid eats these veggie-loaded burgers with "healthy" enthusiasm.

Just Beet It Turkey Burgers

24+ MONTHS

MAKES 2 adult and 2 kid-size patties
PREP TIME: 10 minutes
COOK TIME: 5 minutes

STORAGE
Refrigerator: 3 days

2 tablespoons peeled and grated red beet

2 tablespoons peeled and grated golden beet

1 pound ground turkey meat

1 medium-sized carrot, peeled and grated

1 tablespoon chopped fresh cilantro

2 tablespoons Greek yogurt

Sea salt

Freshly ground black pepper

4 buns or rolls of your choosing

4 leaves of lettuce, torn

1 large tomato, sliced

1 medium onion, sliced into rings

Heat a grill or a large grill pan over medium-high heat until hot.

Place the grated beets between a couple layers of paper towels to soak up any moisture. Repeat the process until the paper towels do not have much color left from the beets.

In a medium bowl, combine the turkey, beets, carrot, cilantro, and yogurt, mixing together with your hands. Add a good pinch of salt and pepper.

Form the turkey mixture into 2 big patties and 2 small patties.

Place the turkey patties on the grill, and cook for 5 minutes on each side or until done. The beets will slightly discolor the turkey meat, so keep that in mind when cooking.

Let sit for 3 to 5 minutes.

Serve each burger on a bun. For the smaller patties, you'll want to remove the excess bun or forego the bun altogether.

Top each burger with lettuce, tomato, and onion, or substitute these with your favorite fixings.

TIP Let the beets inspire you to make a light side salad for the adults. Grate 2 beets and 2 carrots, and mix in 3 to 4 tablespoons of olive oil, ¼ cup of crumbled goat cheese, and 1 tablespoon of toasted pumpkin seeds.

Do you ever try to feed your child bites of the food that you are eating and pass it off as their dinner? If yours is at all like mine, bites of food are now refused. "Whole thing," is what my toddler wants. Just watch your little one's eyes go wide when you make her dreams come true by putting a whole pot pie *in her hand*. My own recipe seasons the traditional pot pie mixture with thyme and Dijon mustard. From start to finish, these comforting pies will be in your toddler's hands in less than an hour, and polished off in a matter of minutes.

Chicken "Hand" Pot Pies

24+ MONTHS

MAKES 8 (2 pie) servings
PREP TIME: 15 minutes
COOK TIME: 45 minutes

STORAGE
Refrigerator: 3 days
Freezer: 2 months

1 tablespoon butter

½ onion, chopped

1 carrot, peeled and chopped

1 stalk celery, chopped

Salt

Freshly ground black pepper

1 garlic clove, minced

1 teaspoon dried thyme

1 teaspoon dried parsley

1 tablespoon whole-wheat flour

1 cup chicken stock

1 teaspoon Dijon mustard

¼ cup peas, frozen

¼ cup corn, frozen

1½ cups cubed cooked chicken

2 packages whole-wheat biscuit dough

Preheat the oven to 375°F. Line a baking sheet with parchment paper or a silicon mat.

In a large skillet, melt the butter over medium heat. Stir in the onion, carrot, and celery; season with salt and pepper; and cook for 10 minutes, or until tender, stirring occasionally. Add the garlic, thyme, and parsley, and cook for an additional minute.

Add the flour and stir until everything is incorporated. Turn up the heat to medium-high, and add the stock and Dijon mustard, stirring until everything is incorporated.

Turn down the heat to low, add the peas, corn, and chicken, and cook for 5 to 10 minutes. Remove and let cool slightly.

CONTINUED

CHICKEN "HAND" POT PIES

....

continued

On a lightly floured surface, take the biscuit dough and spread out each biscuit with the palm of your hand until you get a 5-inch circle. Spoon 2 big tablespoons of the chicken mixture into half of the dough, fold the dough in half over the filling, and using a fork, press the edges and seal.

Place each hand pie onto the baking sheet, and cook for 20 to 25 minutes or until golden brown.

Let cool for 10 minutes, as the insides will be very hot, and serve.

COCKTAIL PAIRING TIP Once your child is asleep and you're headed back to the kitchen for another pot pie, it's easy to make the perfect cocktail accompaniment: Blushing Whiskey Sour. Grab your cocktail shaker and add 3 blackberries, 1 ounce simple syrup, 1 ounce lemon juice, 1 ounce whisky, and 1 cup crushed ice, and shake vigorously until the black berries are broken up. Strain over a glass packed with fresh ice. Garnish with a lemon swirl and blackberry.

Stay with me here, fellow parents. I didn't dream up this recipe to test the limits of what a child is willing to try. Sure, I had my doubts about how well it'd go over, but I'm happy to report that it's in this book for a reason—it's a winner. Thin, buttery pieces of naan flatbread are precooked for extra crispiness, then topped with a creamy peanut butter coconut curry sauce. Add some veggies (those in the recipe are what I used, but anything you have in your fridge will do) sliced long and thin. The mozzarella cheese is a must, while the feta and cilantro add some zing.

Coconut Curry Veggies on Naan

24+ MONTHS

MAKES 4 individual servings
PREP TIME: 15 minutes
COOK TIME: 15 minutes

STORAGE
Refrigerator: 3 days
Freezer: Not recommended

4 pieces precooked whole-wheat naan flatbread

½ cup creamy peanut butter

½ cup canned coconut milk

1 teaspoon mild curry powder

¼ teaspoon red pepper flakes (optional)

2 teaspoons olive oil

½ cup peeled and shredded carrots

½ cup finely sliced red bell pepper

½ cup small florets broccoli,

1 cup grated mozzarella cheese

2 tablespoons crumbled feta cheese

1 tablespoon finely chopped fresh cilantro

Preheat the oven to 450°F.

Place the naan onto a baking sheet, and heat in the oven for 5 minutes.

In a small bowl, whisk together the peanut butter, coconut milk, curry powder, and pepper flakes.

With a pastry brush, brush each naan with a small amount of olive oil, then evenly spread the curry sauce over each naan.

Sprinkle each naan with the carrots, red pepper, broccoli, mozzarella, and feta.

Bake for 10 minutes or until mozzarella is bubbly and brown. Let cool slightly.

Sprinkle with cilantro and serve.

One January, I decided to leave snowy Chicago to travel around Spain for a month—and, yes, this was way before I had kids or any major responsibilities. Authentic Spanish paella completely stole my heart—its earthy robust smell and soft creamy texture, all mixed with bold seasonings. I loved it all, except the more exotic sea creatures always lurking in there. Since then I have played with various recipes trying to make a paella a bit more kid friendly, using rice, shrimp, spices, and vegetables, all simmered together with a good pinch of saffron. Once you get this basic recipe down, feel free to add any other items in traditional paella: beef, pork, sausage, mussels, squid, or clams.

Shrimp Paella

24+ MONTHS

MAKES 8 servings
PREP TIME: 10 minutes
COOK TIME: 45 minutes

STORAGE
Refrigerator: 3 days
Freezer: Not recommended

5 cups low-sodium chicken broth

1 teaspoon crushed saffron threads

2 tablespoons olive oil

½ pound boneless, skinless chicken thighs, trimmed and cut into 1-inch pieces

1 tablespoon smoked paprika

3 bay leaves

3 garlic cloves, minced

2 tomatoes, cored and diced

1 yellow onion, finely chopped

Salt

Freshly ground black pepper

2 cups paella or short-grain rice

½ cup chopped fresh parsley

1 lemon, juiced, divided

1 large roasted red bell pepper from a jar, drained and thinly sliced

1 cup peas, frozen

½ pound shrimp, peeled and deveined

In a small saucepan, bring ½ cup of broth to a simmer over medium, add saffron, remove from heat, and let soak for 10 minutes.

In a large, deep skillet, or paella pan, heat the olive oil over medium-high heat. Add the chicken, and cook for 5 to 7 minutes or until lightly browned.

Add the paprika, bay leaves, garlic, tomatoes, onion, season with salt and pepper, and let cook for 10 minutes, stirring frequently.

Add the saffron broth and remaining 4½ cups chicken broth, and bring to a boil. Stir in the rice, parsley, and half of the lemon juice.

Top with the peppers and peas, and cook, without stirring, for 15 to 20 minutes, or until most of the liquid has been absorbed. Reduce heat to medium-low, and add shrimp, pressing them into the rice mixture; cook for 6 to 8 minutes, or until the shrimp are cooked.

Sprinkle with the remaining half of the lemon juice, and remove from heat. Cover with a towel, and let stand for 10 minutes before serving.

· ·

WINE PAIRING TIP I typically pair my humble seafood paella with an inexpensive white wine, but I also suggest a bubbly Rosé Cava whose faint floral aromatics and spicy fruit undertones pair nicely with this spinach rice dish. An added bonus: you can usually grab a bottle for around $15!

· ·

While I was pregnant with my second child, chicken with udon noodles was a major craving. I would order this dish takeout almost every week, and often Ellie and I would eat it straight from the container. I've worked to come up with a healthier version that matches the great taste we both fell in love with minus the unwanted calories and fat. This version stands up to the test.

Chicken + Udon Noodles
IN GARLIC PEPPER SAUCE
24+ MONTHS

MAKES 4 servings
PREP TIME: 15 minutes
COOK TIME: 25 minutes

STORAGE
Refrigerator: 3 days
Freezer: Not recommended

3 garlic cloves, minced

1-inch piece fresh ginger, grated

3 tablespoons soy sauce

½ cup vegetable or chicken stock

1 tablespoon sesame oil

¼ teaspoon hot sauce

2 tablespoons honey

2 teaspoons freshly ground black pepper

1 (8-ounce) package whole-wheat
   udon noodles

1 tablespoon olive oil

1 pound boneless skinless chicken breast,
   sliced into 1-inch-thick strips

½ cup thinly sliced red bell pepper

½ cup thinly sliced yellow bell pepper

½ cup peeled and sliced carrots

½ cup broccoli florets

1 tablespoon sesame seeds, for serving

In a small bowl, whisk together garlic, ginger, soy sauce, stock, sesame oil, hot sauce, honey, and black pepper. Set aside.

Bring a large pot of water to a boil. Add the noodles, and cook for 2 to 3 minutes, or until noodles are al dente. Drain and rinse in cold water.

In large skillet, heat the olive oil over medium heat. Add the chicken pieces, and cook for 8 minutes, or until lightly browned on all sides.

Add the red and yellow peppers, carrots, and broccoli, and cook, covered, for 5 minutes. Add the noodles and sauce, and stir until everything is well incorporated, and cook for an additional 3 minutes.

Serve and sprinkle with sesame seeds.

BEER PAIRING TIP To match the spiciness from the garlic pepper sauce, pair this dish with a nice IPA like Avery Brewing's India Pale Ale.

I make these teriyaki meatballs for everything—birthday parties, weekday dinners, drop-off meals for new moms. Made with pineapple, soy sauce, and green onions, these meatballs are browned to perfection, then simmered in a tropical, sweet, and slightly spicy sauce (I always add extra hot sauce to my plate) with pineapple and peppers. I haven't yet met a kid who doesn't love this tempting fruity combination. I like to serve this over steamed brown rice mixed with chopped cilantro, a drizzle of olive oil, and a dash of salt and pepper, alongside a simple mixed green salad for the adults.

Teriyaki Meatballs
WITH PINEAPPLE ✚ RED BELL PEPPERS
24+ MONTHS

MAKES 6 small servings
PREP TIME: 15 minutes
COOK TIME: 45 to 120 minutes

STORAGE
Refrigerator: 3 days
Freezer: Not recommended

FOR THE MEATBALLS

Cooking spray

¼ cup panko bread crumbs

1½ pounds ground chicken or beef

2 garlic cloves, minced

1-inch piece fresh ginger, minced

2 teaspoons brown sugar

2 stalks green onions, finely chopped

2 tablespoons soy sauce

¼ cup drained and finely chopped canned pineapple chunks

Salt

Freshly ground black pepper

FOR THE SAUCE

¼ cup brown sugar

3 tablespoons soy sauce

1 tablespoon cornstarch

2 garlic cloves, minced

1 lemon, juiced

1 (20-ounce) can pineapple chunks, divided

1 red bell pepper, seeded and sliced

1 orange bell pepper, seeded and sliced

Preheat the oven to 450°F. Generously spray a baking sheet with cooking spray.

In a medium bowl, mix together the bread crumbs, ground meat, garlic, ginger, brown sugar, green onions, soy sauce, and chopped pineapple with your hands until everything is well incorporated, and season with salt and pepper.

Shape meat mixture into 1-inch balls, and place them on a baking sheet. Bake for 12 to 15 minutes, gently stirring halfway through baking time.

In a large skillet, whisk together the brown sugar, soy sauce, cornstarch, garlic, and lemon juice over medium heat until well combined. Add in the pineapple and bell peppers, and bring to a gentle boil.

Add in the meatballs, reduce heat to the lowest setting, stir every so often, and let it gently simmer for 30 minutes up to 2 hours. The longer you let them cook, the more intense the flavor of the sauce.

COCKTAIL PAIRING TIP When I make these meatballs, I like to treat myself to a drink I came up with on a business trip to Hawaii (rough business trip, I know!)—I named it the Slice of Sunshine. At the bottom of a cocktail shaker, crush ¼ cup pineapple chunks with their juices, then add 1 ounce vodka and ice. Shake and pour everything into a tall glass. Top with soda water, and add 1 cherry to the rim.

This may seem like an exotic soup to make into a toddler recipe, but I find the creamy taste of peanut butter makes my kiddo devour this in no time at all. I also appreciate that this soup is chunky, with less broth than most. I don't know about your kid, but mine tends to be a very messy eater, and when it comes to soup, more of it ends up down her front than in her mouth. So the chunkier the better!

Sweet Potato + Peanut Soup

WITH CHICKEN AND RICE

24+ MONTHS

MAKES 8 servings
PREP TIME: 15 minutes
COOK TIME: 85 minutes

STORAGE
Refrigerator: 3 days
Freezer: Not recommended

2 tablespoons olive oil

1 onion, chopped

2-inch piece of ginger, minced

2 garlic cloves, minced

2 pounds boneless, skinless chicken breasts or thighs, fat trimmed

3 sweet potatoes, peeled and cubed

1 (15-ounce) can of crushed tomatoes

4 cups of low-sodium chicken broth

½ cup creamy peanut butter

1 tablespoon ground coriander

Pinch cayenne pepper

1 cup crushed roasted peanuts

2 cups cooked brown rice

Salt

Freshly ground black pepper

2 tablespoons fresh cilantro, finely chopped

In a large Dutch oven, heat olive oil over medium heat. Add the onion and cook for 3 to 4 minutes or until translucent, stirring occasionally. Add the ginger and the garlic, and cook for another 2 minutes. Add the chicken and cook for 5 to 7 minutes, stirring, or until lightly brown on all sides but not cooked all the way through.

Turn up the heat to medium-high; add the sweet potatoes, tomatoes, chicken broth, peanut butter, coriander, and cayenne pepper; stir well; and bring to a boil. Reduce the heat to low and simmer for 60 minutes.

Remove the chicken pieces, let cool slightly, and cut into bite-size chunks.

Using a stick hand blender or blender, quickly pulse the soup until slightly chunky.

Add the chicken, peanuts, and brown rice to the pot, and cook on low for another 10 to 15 minutes. Season with salt and pepper.

Spoon the soup into individual bowls, and sprinkle with cilantro.

....

TIP One medium sweet potato provides your baby with a daily dose of vitamin A. Sweet potatoes are a great source of beta-carotene, a powerful antioxidant known to give orange vegetables and fruits their vibrant color, which is converted to vitamin A in the body. Consuming foods rich in beta-carotene may also offer your baby protection against asthma.

....

While lying in bed one night dreaming of food (when one is a baby food blogger, this happens more often than normal), I was imagining the delicious combination of roasted sweet potatoes and spinach, which turned into questioning how to add this to a carb, leading of course to considering what cheese could best top this off. And thus these savory lasagna roll-ups were born. Sweet, creamy, and filled with healthy nutrients, this version of lasagna won't kill your waistline or make you feel guilty (alright, not much)—it's all about health here.

Sweet Potato Lasagna Roll-Ups + Spinach + Ricotta

24+ MONTHS

MAKES 6 (2 roll) servings
PREP TIME: 20 minutes
COOK TIME: 70 minutes

STORAGE
Refrigerator: 3 days
Freezer: 1 month, defrost before baking

12 uncooked lasagna noodles

4 medium sweet potatoes,
    peeled and cubed

2 cups ricotta cheese

1 (10-ounce) package frozen chopped
    spinach, thawed and squeezed dry

¼ cup grated Parmesan (plus more
    for serving)

1 garlic clove, minced

¼ teaspoon ground nutmeg

¼ teaspoon onion powder

¼ teaspoon salt

½ teaspoon freshly ground black pepper

3 tablespoons olive oil

2 cups shredded mozzarella cheese

Preheat the oven to 375°F.

Bring a large pot of salted water to a boil, and cook the lasagna noodles according to package directions. Drain and set aside

Bring a medium pot of water to a boil, add the sweet potatoes, and cook for 20 to 30 minutes or until potatoes are tender. Drain and let cool in a medium bowl. When cool enough to handle, mash with a potato masher or fork.

In a food processor or blender, add the ricotta cheese, spinach, ¼ cup Parmesan, garlic, nutmeg, onion powder, salt, and pepper and purée until all increments are combined and slightly chunky, scraping down sides if needed.

CONTINUED

SWEET POTATO LASAGNA ROLL-UPS + SPINACH + RICOTTA

continued

Lay out a lasagna noodle, and spread ⅓ cup or enough mashed sweet potato to cover the entire noodle. Next spread ⅓ cup or enough cheese mixture over noodles, and carefully roll up. Place rolled-up lasagna noodle, seam-side down, into a 9-by-13 baking dish.

Repeat process until all the noodles have been used. Generously brush the top of each lasagna roll with olive oil, then sprinkle with mozzarella cheese.

Bake for 25 to 30 minutes or until cheese is bubbly and golden brown. Let cool for 10 minutes before serving. Serve with remaining Parmesan cheese.

WINE PAIRING TIP To play against the sweet flavors of the lasagna, a fruity white wine with some acidity is the perfect parent-friendly accompaniment. My favorite is a Sauvignon Blanc from either the Friuli or Emilia-Romagna regions of Italy.

This is a warm and comforting soup I like to make when someone in my house is under the weather and needs a little extra love, which in snowy Colorado happens often! One night when my husband was sick, I started to make my usual chicken noodle soup, but soon realized I was out of both chicken and noodles. So instead of scrapping the whole project and serving up canned soup, I reached into the freezer and found some cheese tortellini, instantly giving my classic soup a twist. While this is a vegetarian version of the recipe, feel free to add 1 to 2 cups of cooked chicken.

Comforting Cheese Tortellini Soup

24+ MONTHS

MAKES 6 servings
PREP TIME: 10 minutes
COOK TIME: 30 minutes

STORAGE
Refrigerator: 3 days
Freezer: Not recommended

6 cups low-sodium chicken or vegetable broth

½ large onion, chopped

3 stalks celery, finely chopped

3 large carrots, peeled and finely chopped

1 tablespoon tomato paste

1 teaspoon dried basil

½ teaspoon dried oregano

2 teaspoons dried parsley

½ teaspoon freshly ground black pepper

1 package (9 ounces) refrigerated cheese tortellini

In a large pot over high heat, bring the broth to a boil, then reduce heat to low and simmer.

Add the onion, celery, carrots, tomato paste, dried basil, dried oregano, dried parsley, and pepper, and simmer for 15 minutes, or until carrots are tender, stirring occasionally.

Add in the package of tortellini, and cook for another 10 minutes. Let cool slightly and serve.

Baked sweet potatoes are not only extremely easy to make, but there are a million toppings you can add to keep this healthy recipe new and exciting. To get my toddler involved with making her own food, I prep all the ingredients and then let her build her own sweet potato. Since I know there will be at least a couple of nutritious options followed by some fun ones, I know she'll be getting a wholesome meal no matter how many bacon crumbles she adds on top.

DIY Baked Sweet Potato Bar

24+ MONTHS

MAKES 4 servings
PREP TIME: 15 minutes
COOK TIME: 45 minutes

STORAGE
Refrigerator: 3 days
Freezer: Not recommended

FOR BAKED SWEET POTATO

4 medium sweet potatoes

Prick the sweet potatoes several times with a fork and place on a baking sheet. Roast in the oven for 45 to 50 minutes or until tender. Let them cool slightly.

TIP I have found that my toddler enjoys cooking with me more when she has her own apron and step stool—an easy (and cute) request I was happy to supply to bring her into the kitchen.

MEDITERRANEAN

1 tablespoon olive oil

¼ cup sliced black olives

¼ cup drained and thinly sliced oil-packed sun-dried tomatoes

¼ cup chopped fresh parsley

½ cup crumbled feta cheese

Divide all the ingredients between the 4 cooked sweet potatoes, broil for 5 minutes, or until cheese is melted, and serve.

MANGO-LICIOUS

1 (15-ounce) can black beans, drained and rinsed

1 mango, peeled, pitted, and diced

1 tomato, chopped

1 jalapeño, minced

2 tablespoons finely chopped red onion

2 tablespoons finely chopped cilantro

1 lime, juiced

1 tablespoon olive oil

Mix all the ingredients together, divide between the 4 cooked sweet potatoes, and serve.

MIDWESTERN CHILI

2 tablespoons butter

1 can favorite chili, turkey, beef, or black bean, warmed

½ cup sour cream

1 cup grated Cheddar cheese

2 tablespoons chopped fresh cilantro

Divide the ingredients between the 4 cooked sweet potatoes, broil for 5 minutes, or until the cheese is melted. Sprinkle with cilantro.

BALT

4 slices bacon, cooked and crumbled

1 avocado, peeled, seeded, and chopped

2 cups thinly sliced romaine lettuce

1 tomato, chopped

2 tablespoons ranch dressing

Divide the ingredients between the 4 cooked sweet potatoes, drizzle with ranch dressing, and serve.

When we go Grammy's house (yes—that'd be my mom's) for dinner, she usually ends up making her chicken enchiladas—the dish Ellie and I request the most. These simple enchiladas are an example of why sometimes less is actually more. What takes these humble enchiladas to the next level is my mom's homemade sauce, made from fresh green tomatillos. The result is a simply delicious, deeply flavored meal enjoyable to all generations.

Grammy's Green Tomatillo + Chicken Enchiladas

24+ MONTHS

MAKES 6 servings
PREP TIME: 25 minutes
COOK TIME: 60 minutes

STORAGE
Refrigerator: 3 days
Freezer: 2 months

FOR THE ENCHILADAS

Cooking spray

3 boneless, skinless chicken breasts

Salt (as seasoning, plus 1 teaspoon)

Freshly ground black pepper

⅓ cup half-and-half

4 ounces cream cheese, softened

1 small onion, finely chopped

1 teaspoon ground cumin

½ teaspoon garlic powder

Pinch cayenne pepper

8 (8-inch) corn or flour tortillas

¾ cup shredded Cheddar cheese

¾ cup shredded Monterey Jack cheese

2 tablespoons finely chopped cilantro
(for serving)

2 tablespoons sour cream (for serving)

1 tomato, chopped (for serving)

FOR THE ENCHILADA SAUCE

12 tomatillos, husked

4 serrano peppers, stemmed, seeded,
and minced

3 cups low-sodium chicken broth

2 tablespoons cornstarch

1 teaspoon salt

¼ cup chopped fresh cilantro

CONTINUED

GRAMMY'S GREEN TOMATILLO + CHICKEN ENCHILADAS

continued

Preheat the oven to 350°F. Line a baking sheet with foil.

Season the chicken breasts with salt and pepper, and bake on the baking sheet for 20 minutes, or until cooked through. Let cool and shred.

In a large bowl, mix the half-and-half and the cream cheese until smooth and fluffy. Stir in the chicken, onion, cumin, garlic powder, cayenne pepper, and 1 teaspoon salt. Set aside.

In a medium saucepan, bring tomatillos, peppers, and chicken broth to a boil for 10 minutes. Dissolve cornstarch in 3 tablespoons of cold water. Add cornstarch, salt, and cilantro to the boiling broth, and let boil for 5 more minutes. Remove from the heat, and let cool slightly.

In a blender or food processor, add tomatillo sauce and purée until smooth.

Spray a 9-by-13-inch baking dish with cooking spray, and pour a thin layer of tomatillo sauce into the dish.

Heat tortillas in batches in the microwave for 20 to 30 seconds, or until easy to wrap.

On each tortilla, spoon ½ cup of chicken in a line down the center. Gently roll and place in the baking dish, seam-side down. Repeat until all of the tortillas and chicken mixture is used up.

Spoon the remaining tomatillo sauce over the tortillas.

Cover with foil and bake for 25 to 30 minutes or until hot throughout. Remove the foil, sprinkle with the cheeses, and bake for another 10 minutes or until the cheese is melted and golden brown. Let cool for 10 minutes before serving.

Serve with a sprinkle of cilantro, a dollop of sour cream, and a few tomato chunks.

Getting picky eaters to eat fish can sometimes be a feat (especially if it isn't breaded and fried), but having them grow up eating fish is important because it's jam-packed in omega-3s that help with brain development. While tender and juicy on the inside, this salmon has a tasty honey and ginger glaze that gives it a slightly crunchy crust—something I have found few toddlers can resist.

Honey-Ginger Baked Salmon

24+ MONTHS

MAKES 4 servings
PREP TIME: 10 minutes
COOK TIME: 20 minutes

STORAGE
Refrigerator: 3 days
Freezer: Not recommended

1-inch piece fresh ginger, minced

1 garlic clove, minced

3 tablespoons soy sauce

3 tablespoons squeezed orange juice

3 tablespoons honey

Freshly ground black pepper

1 pound salmon fillet

Preheat the oven to 400°F.

In a small bowl, mix the ginger, garlic, soy sauce, orange juice, honey, and pepper.

In a shallow glass baking dish, place the salmon, and coat with the honey-ginger glaze. Cover the dish, and let it marinate in the refrigerator for 30 minutes, turning once.

Place the baking dish in the oven, and bake, uncovered, for 15 minutes, or until you can easily flake the fish with a fork. For a crispy crust, turn the oven to broil, and cook for an additional 5 minutes.

Let cool slightly and serve. You might want to remove the skin for your toddler.

TIP I like to serve this with steamed green asparagus and cooked barley for a well-rounded and tasty family dinner.

These chicken taquitos are perfect in every way. Rolled tortillas are baked until golden and crispy on the outside, while inside, gooey, melt-in-your-mouth cheesy chicken is immersed in chipotle-chili flavor. Though most people shy away from giving their toddlers a bit of spice, I find that most kids love a little heat in their food.

Baked Chicken + Chipotle Taquitos

24+ MONTHS

MAKES 6 (2-taquito) servings
PREP TIME: 15 minutes
COOK TIME: 20 minutes

STORAGE
Refrigerator: 3 days
Freezer: 2 months

2 cups shredded cooked chicken

2 ounces cream cheese

1 cup shredded sharp white
    Cheddar cheese

3 tablespoons chipotle salsa

1 teaspoon ground cumin

½ teaspoon garlic powder

2 tablespoons chopped fresh cilantro

Juice of 1 lime

Salt

Freshly ground black pepper

12 (8-inch) tortillas of choice

Cooking spray or 1 tablespoon olive oil

Preheat the oven to 400°F. Line a baking sheet with foil.

Soak 12 toothpicks in a small bowl of water.

In a medium pan, add the chicken, cream cheese, cheese, salsa, cumin, garlic powder, cilantro, and lime juice. Heat on medium heat until the cheese has melted and all of the ingredients are well incorporated.

Season with salt and pepper.

Wrap a few tortillas at a time in damp paper towels, and heat them in the microwave for 20 to 30 seconds, or until the tortillas can roll without cracking.

Place 1 tortilla in front of you, and fill it with 2 to 3 tablespoons of the filling. Tightly roll the tortilla and place it seam-side down on a baking sheet. If your tortilla starts to unroll, stick a toothpick into it before baking.

Spray the taquitos with cooking spray or brush with olive oil.

Bake for 15 to 20 minutes or until golden brown.

Let cool for 5 to 10 minutes and remove toothpicks before serving.

TIP It's a great idea to make a double batch and freeze half of the taquitos before baking them—that way you can easily have a healthy meal another day when you're tight on time. Just take the taquitos out of freezer, place them on a baking sheet, and bake at 400°F for 20 to 25 minutes.

Who says toddlers can't enjoy sushi? Letting older toddlers build their own sushi rolls is a fun (and totally messy) way to get their little fingers going in the kitchen. The rolls will not be perfect, or anywhere close to it, but it doesn't matter. Providing a big assortment of finely sliced ingredients will give even the pickiest eaters a chance to try something new. I like to get all the ingredients prepped while my toddler pretends to nap, so at dinner time, I can be totally present and participate in all the fun.

DIY Toddler Sushi Bar

24+ MONTHS

MAKES 8 rolls
PREP TIME: 20 + rolling time minutes

STORAGE
Refrigerator: 1 day
Freezer: Not recommended

FOR THE RICE

2 tablespoons rice vinegar

1 tablespoon sugar

1 teaspoon salt

2 cups sushi rice, cooked per package instructions and cooled

FILLING OPTIONS

1 carrot, peeled and finely sliced

1 avocado, peeled, pitted, and finely sliced

1 red bell pepper, seeded, and finely sliced

4 strawberries, trimmed, and finely sliced

¼ cup finely sliced pineapple chunks

½ cucumber, seeded, finely sliced

2 tablespoons pickled Japanese eggplant

FOR THE SUSHI

8 toasted nori seaweed sheets

Bamboo rolling mat

1 tablespoon rice wine vinegar

Soy sauce, for serving

Pickled ginger, for serving

Combine the rice vinegar, sugar, and salt in a small bowl, and heat in the microwave for 30 to 45 seconds, or until the sugar has dissolved.

In a large mixing bowl, add the rice and vinegar mixture. Fold together until well combined, and let cool to room temperature before you start making the sushi.

On the counter, have all of your sushi making items ready before the rolling begins: nori, bamboo mat, small bowl of rice wine vinegar, and fillings.

CONTINUED

DIY TODDLER SUSHI BAR

. . . .

continued

Select one sheet of nori and place the shiny side down onto the bamboo mat. Wet your hands with vinegar, pick up ⅓ cup of rice, and spread onto the bottom ⅓ of nori, about ¼-inch thick.

Add your fillings in the center of the rice, and gently press down. This is a great step for your toddler to join in on, but don't pile fillings too high or it will become hard to roll.

Gently roll by lifting the bamboo mat nearest to you and fold over the ingredients, lifting it off the nori as you roll. Dip your fingers into the vinegar, and wet the top of the nori sheet, rolling the nori all the way to the top to seal the roll closed. Roll it back and forth several times between the bamboo mat to ensure that it has sealed.

Unwrap the roll from the bamboo mat, and cut into 8 even slices with a sharp knife.

Serve with soy sauce and pickled ginger.

. . . .

TIP Like other vegetables, seaweed, or "vegetables from the sea," contains essential vitamins and minerals, including your baby's daily dose of iodine, a mineral that is critical for healthy thyroid function.

. . . .

You'll be hard pressed to find a toddler who doesn't go crazy over sloppy joes! I think even my husband could live off of these for weeks at a time. While still a little messy—isn't that part of the fun?—these vegan sloppy joes are made with crumbled tempeh and loaded with red and green bell peppers, corn, and zucchini. And being free of meat, dairy, nuts, and gluten, you won't find a tastier and easier allergy-free option to serve at your next toddler get together.

Vegan Veggie-Loaded Sloppy Joes

24+ MONTHS

MAKES 6 servings
PREP TIME: 10 minutes
COOK TIME: 15 minutes

STORAGE
Refrigerator: 3 days
Freezer: Not recommended

2 tablespoons olive oil

2 (8-ounce) packages of tempeh, crumbled

½ onion, chopped

1 garlic clove, minced

½ red bell pepper, chopped

½ green bell pepper, chopped

1 small zucchini, chopped

½ cup corn, fresh or frozen

1 can tomato sauce

1 tablespoon brown sugar

1 tablespoon yellow mustard

½ teaspoon ground cumin

½ teaspoon ground coriander

½ teaspoon dried oregano

½ teaspoon dried parsley

¼ teaspoon paprika

Pinch cayenne pepper

Salt

Freshly ground black pepper

6 hamburger buns, whole-wheat or gluten-free, toasted

2 tablespoons mayonnaise

12 slices dill pickles (optional)

In a large skillet, heat the olive oil over medium heat. Add the tempeh and cook, stirring, for 5 to 10 minutes or until browned. Add in the onion and cook for another 3 minutes. Add in the garlic, red pepper, green pepper, zucchini, and corn, and cook for 3 to 5 minutes, stirring occasionally.

Stir in the tomato sauce, brown sugar, mustard, cumin, coriander, dried oregano, dried parsley, paprika, and cayenne pepper, and season with salt and pepper. Bring to a slight boil. Reduce heat and simmer, stirring occasionally, for 10 to 15 minutes.

To serve, spread the mayonnaise on the buns, spoon tempeh mixture evenly onto the buns, and top with pickles.

Fish tacos are the perfect meal to end a hot summer day. This is our go-to fish taco recipe because it combines three out of four of my favorite things: crispy fish, pineapple salsa, and freshly sliced avocado. My toddler will devour it as well, which makes it a doubly perfect finish to the day.

Fish Taco + Avocado + Pineapple Salsa

24+ MONTHS

MAKES 4 (2 taco) servings
PREP TIME: 20 minutes
COOK TIME: 10 minutes

STORAGE
Refrigerator: 1 day
Freezer: Not recommended

FOR THE FISH

2 tablespoons olive oil

½ jalapeño pepper, halved lengthwise

1 pound tilapia fillets

Salt

Freshly ground black pepper

FOR THE TACOS

¼ cup sour cream

2 limes, juiced, divided

½ jalapeño, seeded and minced

2 cups finely shredded red cabbage

2 tablespoons olive oil

8 (6-inch) corn or flour tortillas

2 tablespoons chopped fresh cilantro

1 avocado, seeded and sliced

FOR THE PINEAPPLE SALSA

2 cups diced pineapple

2 medium tomatoes, seeded and chopped

½ sweet onion, chopped

1 garlic clove, minced

¼ cup chopped fresh cilantro

1 jalapeño pepper, seeded and chopped

½ teaspoon ground cumin

½ teaspoon salt

In a medium skillet, heat the olive oil and jalapeño pepper over medium heat, swirling the oil to coat the skillet evenly. Season the tilapia fillets with salt and pepper before placing them into the skillet. Cook for 5 to 7 minutes, flipping halfway through cooking time. You may need to do this in two batches. Discard the jalapeño pepper.

In a small bowl, mix together the sour cream, half the lime juice, and the jalapeño pepper.

In a medium bowl, toss the red cabbage, olive oil, and the remaining lime juice.

In a food processor, add together the pineapple, tomatoes, onion, garlic, cilantro, jalapeño pepper, cumin, and salt, and pulse until combined but still chunky, roughly 10 seconds. Transfer the salsa to a serving bowl, and let it sit in the fridge until ready.

Heat the tortillas in a microwave for 20 to 30 seconds or until warm.

Serve the fish in warmed tortillas topped with cabbage slaw, a drizzle of sour cream, a pinch of cilantro, slice of avocado, and a big spoonful of pineapple salsa.

....

WINE PAIRING TIP My fourth favorite thing is an old-lady white wine spritzer. In a wine glass, place 2 slices of orange, and combine a half glass chilled white wine (I recommend Pinot Grigio) with 1 cup soda water. Enjoy!

....

Friday night at our house means one thing—pizza night! The ingredients change with the seasons, but this recipe is a staple, with ingredients flavorful and familiar enough to satisfy both the adults and the toddler. It doesn't hurt that Ellie gets invested early on by stretching the dough (and tasting all of the ingredients along the way). If you're really feeling adventurous, top the pizza with chopped spinach or kale, but it is Friday, after all—serious veggies are optional. The homemade crust recipe below is adapted from one of my favorite family blogs, *Two Peas & Their Pod*.

Summer Hatch Green Chile Pizza + Corn + Chicken Sausage

24+ MONTHS

MAKES 1 (8-slice) pizza
PREP TIME: 15 minutes
COOK TIME: 40 minutes

STORAGE
Refrigerator: 3 days

FOR THE CRUST

1 cup warm water (110°F)

1 (¼ ounce) active dry yeast packet

1 teaspoon granulated sugar

1½ cups whole-wheat flour

1 cup white whole-wheat flour

2 tablespoons olive oil, divided

1 tablespoon honey

1 tablespoon dried cilantro, or other favorite spice

1½ teaspoons salt

FOR THE PIZZA

2 tablespoons olive oil, divided

1 large chicken sausage link, Italian flavored

1 teaspoon garlic powder

½ teaspoon red pepper flakes

Sea salt

Freshly ground black pepper

1 cup corn, from cob, can, or frozen

3 tablespoons chopped Hatch green chile, fresh, roasted, or canned

¾ cup shredded sharp white Cheddar cheese

¾ cup shredded Colby-Jack cheese

3 green onions, white and light green parts chopped

CONTINUED

SUMMER HATCH GREEN CHILE PIZZA + CORN + CHICKEN SAUSAGE

continued

TO MAKE THE CRUST

In a medium bowl, combine warm water, yeast, and sugar. Gently stir and let sit for 5 to 10 minutes or until the yeasts starts to bubble.

Add the flours, 1 tablespoon of olive oil, the honey, dried cilantro, and salt. Mix well.

Pour the contents of the bowl onto a lightly floured counter. Knead the dough for 2 to 3 minutes or until the dough forms a ball and is shiny and smooth.

In the medium bowl, add the remaining tablespoon of olive oil, and generously coat all sides.

Place the dough ball into the greased bowl, cover loosely with a damp towel, and let rise for 30 minutes.

TO MAKE THE PIZZA

Preheat the oven to 400ºF.

Roll or stretch the dough into a circle, and place on a pizza stone or pan. For an extra crispy crust, bake the dough in the oven for 8 to 10 minutes or until the dough is just starting to brown.

While the crust is baking, heat 1 tablespoon of olive oil in a medium pan over medium heat. Slice the sausage casing open and remove the meat. Discard the casing. Transfer the meat to the pan, and cook for 8 minutes, breaking up the meat with the back of a wooden spoon.

Brush the pizza crust with the remaining tablespoon of olive oil, and sprinkle it with garlic powder, red pepper flakes, and season with salt and pepper.

Arrange the sausage, corn, and chile on the pizza crust. Sprinkle the cheese evenly onto the pizza.

Turn up the oven to 525°F, or as high as your oven will go.

Cook the pizza for 10 minutes, or until the cheese is bubbly and brown.

Sprinkle the green onions onto the pizza while the cheese is still extremely hot.

Let cool for 5 minutes.

Cut into toddler-size slices and serve.

TIP This recipe calls for homemade pizza dough, though premade dough (and even premade crusts) is widely available in supermarkets and would substitute well for homemade. While I have used premade crusts, there is nothing better to me than my own dough. With only a 30-minute rise time, I find the extra minutes are well worth it.

Frittatas are a quick and easy dish you can whip up either for breakfast or dinner in no time at all. While you can use whichever vegetables and cheese you have in the fridge, this is my family's favorite combo: crispy red peppers, creamy feta, and a handful of spinach (finely chopped so as not to freak out the toddler) for a pop of color and nutrients. Maybe the best part about making a frittata for dinner is you already know what's for breakfast tomorrow morning!

Red Bell Pepper + Feta Frittata with Spinach

24+ MONTHS

MAKES 8 servings
PREP TIME: 10 minutes
COOK TIME: 25 minutes

STORAGE
Refrigerator: 3 days
Freezer: Not recommended

8 eggs

Salt

Freshly ground black pepper

1 tablespoon olive oil

1 small onion, chopped

1 red bell pepper, seeded and thinly sliced

1 cup trimmed and finely chopped packed spinach

½ cup crumbled feta cheese

2 tablespoons chopped chives

TIP Frittatas also make for wonderful salad add-ins. Just chop it up and toss the pieces cold into a simple salad of arugula, avocado, cucumbers, and salsa.

Preheat the broiler.

In a medium bowl, whisk the eggs, and season with salt and pepper. Set aside.

In a large oven-safe skillet, heat the olive oil over medium heat. Add the onion and the pepper and cook for 4 minutes. Add the spinach, and cook for another 2 minutes, stirring occasionally, or until the spinach is just starting to wilt.

Pour in the egg mixture, top with the feta cheese, and cook for 5 to 7 minutes, or until the eggs are set on the bottom and just setting on the top.

Place the skillet in the oven, and broil for 3 to 5 minutes, or until lightly brown and fluffy. Let cool slightly.

Sprinkle with chives and serve in wedges.

I promise you this will be your new go-to pancake recipe. While the pancakes are made with whole-wheat flour and quinoa, they are still fluffy and tender. I add a little Greek yogurt for some extra protein, plus a grated apple for a boost in taste and moistness. If you don't have any cooked quinoa on hand, simply sub in some old-fashion oats for the same great result.

Fluffy Apple + Quinoa Pancakes

24+ MONTHS

MAKES 8 medium pancakes
PREP TIME: 5 minutes
COOK TIME: 20 minutes

STORAGE
Refrigerator: 3 days
Freezer: 2 months

1 large egg

1 cup milk

2 tablespoons brown sugar

¼ cup plain Greek yogurt

1 teaspoon vanilla extract

1 cup whole-wheat flour

½ cup quinoa, cooked and cooled

2 teaspoons baking powder

1 teaspoon ground cinnamon

¼ teaspoon ground nutmeg

¼ teaspoon salt

½ cup apple (roughly 1 apple), grated

Cooking spray or oil

TIP Quinoa is naturally gluten-free and contains iron, B-vitamins, magnesium, phosphorus, potassium, calcium, vitamin E, and fiber. It is one of only a few plant foods considered a complete protein.

In a medium bowl, whisk together the egg and milk. Stir in the brown sugar, yogurt, and vanilla extract until smooth.

Gently stir in the flour, quinoa, baking powder, cinnamon, nutmeg, and salt until just combined.

Add in the grated apple, and stir a couple times, making sure not to overmix.

Heat a griddle or large skillet over medium heat, and generously spray with cooking spray or oil. Pour ¼ cup of batter onto the skillet, cooking for 3 to 5 minutes or until you see small bubbles along the edges of the pancakes. Flip and cook for another 3 minutes, or until golden brown.

Coat the griddle or skillet again, and repeat the process until you have used up all of the batter.

You can keep the pancakes warm in a pre-heated 200°F oven.

Whenever I have book club with my girlfriends (where reading a book is completely optional), I like to leave a premade meal for my family. It's not that my husband isn't capable of getting the girls fed—it's just that I know he'll take them to the beer garden down the street, where ice cream is free for kids every weeknight. Once in a while, sure, but the man is drawn to this place like a magnet. To keep the fam happy and well fed at home, this is one of their all-time favorites recipes—in fact, I am pretty sure they'd send me off to book club every night of the week, as long as they'd get to eat these yummy pizza pockets.

Dad's Night In–Barbecue Chicken + Corn Pizza Pockets

24+ MONTHS

MAKES 8 small pizza pockets
PREP TIME: 20 minutes
COOK TIME: 15 minutes

STORAGE
Refrigerator: 3 days
Freezer: Not recommended

Cooking spray

1 serving fresh pizza dough, store-bought or homemade, at room temperature

½ cup favorite barbecue sauce

½ cup cubed cooked chicken,

2 slices bacon, cooked and crumbled

½ cup corn, thawed if using frozen

½ cup chopped red bell pepper

3 tablespoons finely chopped cilantro leaves

1 cup grated Cheddar cheese or Mexican cheese blend

Preheat the oven to 450°F. Lightly grease a baking sheet with cooking spray

Divide the pizza dough into 8 different balls. On a floured counter, roll each ball into a rectangle shape.

On half of each rectangle shape, leaving an inch around all sides, evenly spoon barbecue sauce over the dough, then evenly sprinkle the chicken, bacon, corn, red pepper, cilantro, and cheese onto each of the pizzas.

Fold dough in half over the filling, and using a fork, press edges together until sealed tight. For a little fun, I like to cut each person's initial into the top of each crust.

Place the pizza pockets onto a baking sheet and bake for 10 to 15 minutes, or until crust is golden brown.

The key to this sandwich's goodness is the homemade breakfast sausage, the cooked egg, the melty cheese . . . oh, fine, to be honest, it's really the sausage. Mixed with a hint of maple syrup and a dash of cumin and sage, these patties have just the right sweet and savory combination we crave in a breakfast meat.

Sweet + Savory Chicken Sausage Breakfast Sandwich

24+ MONTHS

MAKES 4 servings
PREP TIME: 5 minutes
COOK TIME: 15 minutes

STORAGE
Refrigerator: 3 days
Freezer: Not recommended

½ pound ground chicken

1 tablespoon maple syrup

1 teaspoon salt, plus more for seasoning

½ teaspoon freshly ground black pepper, plus more for seasoning

½ teaspoon ground cumin

½ teaspoon ground sage

¼ teaspoon red pepper flakes

Cooking spray or oil

4 large eggs

4 whole-wheat English muffins, halved

4 tablespoons butter

4 slices Swiss or Cheddar cheese

1 avocado, pitted and sliced

In a medium bowl, mix together the chicken, maple syrup, salt, pepper, cumin, sage, and red pepper flakes, and form into 4 patties.

Spray or oil a large skillet over medium-high heat. Place the patties in a skillet, and cook for 3 to 4 minutes per side, or until brown and done in the middle. Place the patties onto a paper-towel-lined plate to drain any excess fat.

Reduce the heat to medium and fry each egg, seasoning with salt and pepper, for 1 to 2 minutes, or until the whites are barely set. Flip the eggs, and cook for an additional 1 to 2 minutes, or until the whites are set and the yolks are set but still soft.

Toast the English muffins. Spread butter onto both halves of the English muffins. To assemble, place 1 egg on the bottom of the English muffin, top with a sausage patty, a slice of cheese, avocado, and finally the English muffin top.

Wrap in foil for 2 to 3 minutes to help the cheese melt, or heat in the microwave for 20 to 30 seconds. Serve warm.

ACKNOWLEDGMENTS

Big hug to my amazing editor, Stacy. Thank you for finding me, convincing me, and making me sit down and write this book, even when I had my doubts. Now please get out of my head, thank you very much!

Thank you, Katy, for making this book so beautiful.

A thousand "thank you"s to Rachel, Lindsey, Mary, Hilary, Jen, and Lauren from my baby mama group, for your unconditional support over the last three years. Motherhood would not be the same without you and your amazing babies in my life.

Sara, thank you for always having my back and encouraging me to always be true to myself.

Thank you to Kevin and Gail for your love and support over the years, and for loaning me a super-fancy camera.

To Dave, for always saying yes to my crazy ideas, and somehow making them work.

Mom, I love you truly, madly, deeply—forever and ever—to the moon and back—and then some.

My adventure in baby-food-making would never have started without the constant support from my amazing hubby! You are my rock that gave me the stars.

And finally, a big XOXO to my readers who, like me, are determined to give their babies the best food the world has to offer. Your passion, inspiration, and humor has made my journey in making baby food a great joy.

—*Michele Olivier*

First, I offer heartfelt gratitude to Michele. Thank you for your continual creativity and inspiration, and for inviting me along for the ride! I would also like to thank all of the teachers, mentors, peers, and students I have had over the years at the Nutrition Therapy Institute for your passion and community. Thank you to all of my beloved clients, for teaching me so much and for raising your beautifully healthy families. Thank you to my friends who cheered us on in the creation of this book. To my husband, Mark, and my kids, Clay and Molly, and to my extended family, as well, thank you for believing in me.

—*Sara Peternell, MNT*

ABOUT THE AUTHORS

Michele Olivier is a mother of two and the founder and author of the popular baby food blog *Baby FoodE*. Her recipes have been featured online on BuzzFeed, PopSugar, Red Tricycle, and Daily Parent, among others. She and her family live in Denver, Colorado.

Follow her online: babyfoode.com

 @babyfoode

 facebook.com/babyfoode

Sara Peternell, MNT, is a nutrition therapist who works with clients primarily for fertility, pregnancy, and postpartum nutrition, as well as in the area of nutrition for young children. She is also an instructor at the Nutrition Therapy Institute. Sara, her husband, and their two children live in Denver, Colorado. More information about her practice can be found online at sarapeternell.com.

THE DIRTY DOZEN & THE CLEAN FIFTEEN

A nonprofit and environmental watchdog organization called Environmental Working Group (EWG) looks at data supplied by the U.S. Department of Agriculture (USDA) and the Food and Drug Administration (FDA) about pesticide residues and compiles a list each year of the best and worst pesticide loads found in commercial crops. You can use these lists to decide which fruits and vegetables to buy organic to minimize your exposure to pesticides and which produce is considered safe enough to skip the organics. This does not mean they are pesticide-free, though, so wash these fruits and vegetables thoroughly.

These lists change every year, so make sure you look up the most recent before you fill your shopping cart. You'll find the most recent lists as well as a guide to pesticides in produce at http://EWG.org/FoodNews.

THE 2015 DIRTY DOZEN

- Apples
- Celery
- Cherry tomatoes
- Cucumbers
- Grapes
- Nectarines
- Peaches
- Potatoes
- Snap peas
- Spinach
- Strawberries
- Sweet bell peppers

Plus produce contaminated with highly toxic organophosphate insecticides:

- Hot peppers
- Kale/collard greens

THE CLEAN FIFTEEN

- Asparagus
- Avocados
- Cabbage
- Cantaloupe
- Cauliflower
- Eggplant
- Grapefruit
- Kiwi
- Mangos
- Onions
- Papayas
- Pineapples
- Sweet corn
- Sweet peas (frozen)
- Sweet potatoes

MEASUREMENT CONVERSIONS

VOLUME EQUIVALENTS (LIQUID)

US STANDARD	US STANDARD (OUNCES)	METRIC (APPROXIMATE)
2 tablespoons	1 fl. oz.	30 mL
¼ cup	2 fl. oz.	60 mL
½ cup	4 fl. oz.	120 mL
1 cup	8 fl. oz.	240 mL
1½ cups	12 fl. oz.	355 mL
2 cups or 1 pint	16 fl. oz.	475 mL
4 cups or 1 quart	32 fl. oz.	1 L
1 gallon	128 fl. oz.	4 L

OVEN TEMPERATURES

FAHRENHEIT (F)	CELSIUS (C) (APPROXIMATE)
250°	120°
300°	150°
325°	165°
350°	180°
375°	190°
400°	200°
425°	220°
450°	230°

VOLUME EQUIVALENTS (DRY)

US STANDARD	METRIC (APPROXIMATE)
⅛ teaspoon	0.5 mL
¼ teaspoon	1 mL
½ teaspoon	2 mL
¾ teaspoon	4 mL
1 teaspoon	5 mL
1 tablespoon	15 mL
¼ cup	59 mL
⅓ cup	79 mL
½ cup	118 mL
⅔ cup	156 mL
¾ cup	177 mL
1 cup	235 mL
2 cups or 1 pint	475 mL
3 cups	700 mL
4 cups or 1 quart	1 L
½ gallon	2 L
1 gallon	4 L

WEIGHT EQUIVALENTS

US STANDARD	METRIC (APPROXIMATE)
½ ounce	15 g
1 ounce	30 g
2 ounces	60 g
4 ounces	115 g
8 ounces	225 g
12 ounces	340 g
16 ounces or 1 pound	455 g

REFERENCES

American Academy of Allergy, Asthsma & Immunology. "Allergy Statistics." http://www.aaaai.org/about-the-aaaai/newsroom/allergy-statistics.aspx.

AskDr.Sears. "Facts about Hydrogenated Fats and Oils." Accessed February 14, 2015. http://www.askdrsears.com/topics/feeding-eating/family-nutrition/facts-about-fats/hydrogenated-fats.

AskDr.Sears. "Juice: The Truth About Pure Fruit Juices vs Fruit Beverages." Accessed February 14, 2015. http://www.askdrsears.com/topics/feeding-eating/family-nutrition/juice.

Bruno, Elizabeth. "10 Processed Foods to Never Feed Your Kids." *Mamavation.* February 9, 2015. Accessed February 15, 2015. http://www.mamavation.com/2015/02/10-processed-foods-never-feed-kids.html.

Chaparro, C. M. "Setting the stage for child health and development: prevention of iron deficiency in early infancy." *The Journal of Nutrition.* 138, no. 12 (Dec 2008): 2529–33.

Enig, Mary. "Dietary Recommendations for Children—A Recipe for Future Heart Disease?" Accessed March 17, 2015. www.westonaprice.org/health-topics/dietary-recommendations-for-children-a-recipe-for-future-heart-disease/

Fallon, Sally. *Nourishing Traditions: The Cookbook That Challenges Politically Correct Nutrition and the Diet Dictocrats.* Washington, DC: NewTrends Publishing, 1999.

Krebs, N. "Research in Progress. Beef as a First Weaning Food." *Food and Nutrition News* 70, no. 2 (1998): 5

Mayo Clinic. "Diseases and Conditions: Anaphylaxis." http://www.mayoclinic.org/diseases-conditions/anaphylaxis/basics/definition/con-20014324.

Scharf, Rebecca J., Ryan T. Demmer, and Mark D. DeBoer. "Longitudinal evaluation of milk type consumed and weight status in preschoolers." *Archives of Disease in Childhood* 2013 doi:10.1136/archdischild-2012-302941; Accessed February 21, 2015. http://adc.bmj.com/content/early/2013/02/13/archdischild-2012-302941.short?g=w_adc_ahead_tab.

INDEX